BURNING BRIDGES

GLEN CAMPBELL

LIFE WITH MY FATHER

BURNING BRIDGES

GLEN CAMPBELL

LIFE WITH MY FATHER

DEBBY CAMPBELL & MARK BEGO

OMNIBUS PRESS

London / New York / Paris / Sydney / Copenhagen / Berlin / Madrid / Tokyo

Cover designed by Fresh Lemon
Picture research by Jacqui Black

ISBN: 978.1.78038.858.8
Order No: OP 55099

Exclusive Distributors
Music Sales Limited,
14/15 Berners Street,
London, W1T 3LJ.

Music Sales Corporation
180 Madison Avenue, 24th Floor,
New York,
NY 10016,
USA.

Macmillan Distribution Services,
56 Parkwest Drive
Derrimut, Vic 3030,
Australia.

All photographs courtesy of the Debby Campbell Collection

Printed in the EU.

A catalogue record for this book is available from the British Library.

Visit Omnibus Press on the web at www.omnibuspress.com

Dedication

To my children Jenny, Jesse and Jeremy; and my grandchildren Morgan, Olive and Micah. I read these words somewhere and they absolutely jumped at me to express how I feel: "I just want you to know that you give me the balance to live right, because so much of what is best in us is bound up in family, that it remains the measure of our stability. You are my heart."

I want you to "never" forget you are family!

Acknowledgements

Debby Campbell would like to thank:

My mom for opening up to me after all these years and telling me her story. I love you.

My stepdad Jack for being the amazing man you are and have always been.

My sisters Donna and Denise for your unconditional love.

MaryAnne Beaman, you are my sister in every sense of that word! I love and adore you! Margaret Cloyd (you are amazing).

Karl Olson.

Venita and Harold Norvell (my uncle passed away on my birthday this year), Jeanne French Newman, Peggy Hobart, Lisa Wopschall, Annie Nouna, Georgia Wright, June Sovay, Carla McCammon, Martha and John Hannah, Lynne O'Leary, Debra Moreno-Lowther, Mae Abner, my family in Arkansas and Texas, Jeanne Lyons Williams, Ron Jacoby, Susan and Gary Andrews, Francine Ventura, Tim and Mary Kimbrell, and my co-writer Mark Bego.

Special love to my Aunt Barbara Frazier whom I look up to with the highest respect and admiration. You have taught me so much all these years and I am so blessed to have your unconditional love. Your entire family glows from within.

My husband Tom: for not giving up on us even when I had, and for loving me when I didn't love myself.

AND TO MY DAD: Thank you for your openness and love. We built such a beautiful friendship out of respect and love. Thank you for some of the most memorable years of my life. This horrible disease is stripping you of your memories. I will hold them in my heart for both of us! I love you.

Mark Bego would like to thank: David Barraclough and Chris Charlesworth, our fantastic editors; MaryAnne Beaman, Mary and Bob Bego, Debby Campbell Cloyd, Tom Cloyd, Dan DiFilippo, Chris Gilman, Suzy Frank,

Frank Hagen, Peter Haury, Randy Jones, Sergio Kardenas, Deborah Moreno-Lowther, Dave Marken, our incredible literally agent Scott Mendel, Nic's Martini Lounge in Beverly Hills, Larry Nicola, Luke Nicola, Michela Nicola, Peter and Aleo in NYC, David Salidor, Carlos Smith, Patrick Wood.

Contents

Prologue: The Daughter Of A Legend, By Mark Bego   11

Introduction: Ghost On The Canvas   17

Chapter One: Mom And Dad   21

Chapter Two: A Child Of Divorce   28

Chapter Three: A Family In Transition   45

Chapter Four: Returning To Dad's Life   51

Chapter Five: Mansion In Branson   55

Chapter Six: The Glen Campbell Goodtime Theater
       And Beyond   63

Chapter Seven: On The Road Again   73

Chapter Eight: By The Time He Got To Scottsdale   78

Chapter Nine: The Best Of Times   87

Chapter Ten: Burning Bridges   98

Chapter Eleven: Unconditional Love   110

Chapter Twelve: These Days   119

Chapter Thirteen: Try A Little Kindness   134

Chapter Fourteen: A Better Place   141

Debby Campbell's Family Tree   159

Glen Campbell's Discography   161

About The Authors   175

The Daughter Of A Legend

by Mark Bego

IT was September 23, 2011, and I was celebrating my birthday in Beverly Hills, California at my favorite nightclub, Nic's Martini Lounge. Three of my friends – Debra Moreno-Lowther, Frank Hagen, and Suzy Frank – came to help me celebrate, and they brought with them a lovely lady I had never met before: Debby Campbell. As we chatted, she told me she was Glen Campbell's oldest daughter, and that after 24 years of singing in her dad's touring concert show, only five days ago she had been unceremoniously fired – due to family politics.

As I sat there listening to an abbreviated cocktail party version of her life story, I knew right then and there that she had a compelling tale to tell, and a book that she needed to write. We made a pact right then and there to put her story on paper. After we formalized our working relationship, we not only began doing taped interviews to get her story down on paper, I also asked her to start a "journal" of her thoughts and feelings as they occurred to her. Debby's "Journal Entries" are some of the most compelling and touching parts of this book.

The finished book that you now hold in your hands is one that is multi-faceted. Not only is it a deeply frank and painfully touching tale of what it was like to grow up with an international superstar as a parent, but it has another very important dynamic as well: as the saga of a child of divorce, and her emotional journey towards building a relationship with an estranged parent. The headline-grabbing revelation of Glen Campbell's June 2011 disclosure that he was suffering from Alzheimer's Disease only makes Debby's story all the more heartfelt and timely.

For me, much of Glen Campbell's music has been part of the

soundtrack of my life, and I am certain that it has been part of yours too. However, as Debby and I started working together, I learned so much more about Glen's life and career, and Debby's pivotal role in it.

In the world of contemporary country music, there are few performers in the last 50 years whose careers have exceeded the accomplishments of Glen Campbell. He first came to prominence in the music business as a recording session guitar player in Los Angeles. As part of the constantly evolving studio band they called the Wrecking Crew, Glen played guitar, Leon Russell was on keyboards, David Gates on bass, and Hal Blaine was on drums. Together, and with additional musicians, they played on hit recordings for a who's who of the recording business, including Elvis Presley, Bobby Darin, Ricky Nelson, Freddy Cannon, Dean Martin, Frank Sinatra, Phil Spector, the Monkees, the Beach Boys, Bobbie Gentry, Anne Murray, Kenny Rogers and Linda Ronstadt.

Signed to his own recording deal in the early sixties at Capital Records, Glen went on to score one hit solo recording after another, including: 'Universal Soldier' (1965), 'Burning Bridges' (1966), 'Gentle On My Mind' (1967), 'By The Time I Get To Phoenix' (1967), 'I Wanna Live' (1968), 'Wichita Lineman' (1968), 'The Dreams Of An Everyday Housewife' (1968), 'Where's The Playground Susie' (1969), 'Try A Little Kindness' (1969) and 'Galveston' (1969).

In 1967 Campbell became the first person to win two Grammy Awards in the Country category and the same night won two Grammys in the Pop category (two Grammys for 'By The Time I Get To Phoenix' and two Grammys for 'Gentle On My Mind'). The following year, album *Gentle On My Mind* won the coveted Grammy Award for Album of the Year.

Then he landed a top-rated primetime TV variety show of his own: *The Glen Campbell Goodtime Hour*, which ran from 1968 to 1972. When he co-starred opposite John Wayne in the 1969 film *True Grit*, Glen became a bona fide movie star.

True Grit was such a big box-office hit that Glen reunited with his female co-star from that film – Kim Darby – to star in the 1970 film *Norwood*. Both of these movies had hit soundtrack albums, and each of these contained new Top 10 singles for Campbell.

While all of this was going on Glen also recorded two very popular duet albums. The first one was with Bobbie Gentry in 1968, which zoomed up to number one on the country charts, and included a pair of hit singles:

'Morning Glory' and 'Let It Be Me'. Gentry and Campbell also scored a subsequent non-album single with the song 'All I Have To Do Is Dream'. In 1971 he recorded a duet album with Anne Murray, which contained the hit single medley of the songs 'I Say A Little Prayer'/'By The Time I Get To Phoenix'. These recordings would later be the basis for Glen to perform these popular duets with his daughter Debby in his concert act.

After Glen's career went through a cooling down phase, a decade after his initial success he returned to the top of the music charts with another impressive string of hits, including 'Rhinestone Cowboy' (1975), 'Country Boy (You Got Your Feet In L.A.)' (1975), and 'Southern Nights' (1977). He is a recording star, a TV star, a concert draw, and a handsome and charismatic movie star. Imagine the excitement of growing up with Glen Campbell as your father! That has been Debby Campbell's life.

As the oldest child from his first marriage in the fifties, Debby's personal journey has been a father and daughter story that is as big and dramatic as Glen Campbell's life has been. Debby has been at his side for some of the biggest triumphs of her father's career, and she has also been by his side for some of the most heartbreaking events in his private life.

Often estranged from her father, Debby watched from the other side of the Atlantic Ocean as he allegedly got into public drunken brawls with his wild country diva girlfriend Tanya Tucker, and ended up on the cover of *The National Enquirer* and *The Star*. Beginning in the late eighties, Debby was part of her dad's stage show and his glory days as the headlining act at several venues, including the Glen Campbell Goodtime Theater in Branson, Missouri. At one point Debby was also Glen's "opening act" when he went out on concert tours. Debby also watched helplessly as her father's life spun out of control, and he was arrested in 2003 on a drunk driving charge. This was an event that caused headline news.

For 24 years, Debby had been by her father's side, singing duets with him as a part of his concert touring show, as well as being a supportive part of his family. Debby has been with her dad through his four wives, through his decades of cocaine and alcohol abuse, and now – as publicly announced in 2011 – through the shattering beginnings of his dealing with Alzheimer's disease.

Acknowledging that he is losing his memory, Glen recorded what were billed as "Glen's Final Studio Albums", *Ghost On The Canvas* (2011) and *See You There* (2013), his show business career is about to come to an end, and his complicated family of children and ex-wives find themselves on opposing sides. Instead of surrounding Glen with a supportive group of professional musician friends for his final three years in the concert spotlight, his fourth wife, Kim, took his career in another direction. In March 2010 Glen's longtime band members were fired. Instead, his final touring musicians were now his own children by fourth wife Kim, plus the kids' fledgling band: Instant People.

Whenever Glen lost his place onstage, Debby had been there to put him back on track. Whenever he needed help on the road or backstage, she was there for him. Since she had been a part of her father's show for 24 years, Debby Campbell had assumed that her position was solid and safe. She was mistaken. On September 18, 2011, Debby was informed by her father's business manager that her services were no longer needed on Glen's international "Goodbye Tour".

Glen's longtime accompanying band had been with him since the eighties, and included Gary Bruzzese (drums), Kenny Skaggs (guitar, steel guitar, mandolin), and Russell Skaggs (bass guitar). The organization also included musical director TJ Kuenster (piano). Debby began singing professionally with her father in 1987.

In the late 2000s things had begun to shift, when Debby's youngest siblings and their band members started playing as part of the act as well. Ashley Campbell started singing and playing guitar with Glen in 2009, and her band Instant People – with brother Cal Campbell and his musician friends Siggy and Ryan – were part of the band as well as of early 2010. Then youngest brother Shannon joined the act. From time to time, record producer Julian Raymond would replace Russell in the show as the guitar player when he elected to do so.

While all of this was going on, Gary, Kenny and Russ were dismissed as Glen's band in March 2010. Debby continued with the act until she was let go in September 2011. From that point, until November 2012 – while the stage act was billed as "The Goodbye Tour," Debby's half-siblings Ashley, Cal, and Shannon Campbell were part of the act as Glen's band without Debby. These many changes led to much confusion both backstage and onstage.

'Burning Bridges' was the first song that Debby Campbell sang professionally with her father onstage, when she became a regular part of his show in 1987. It is also the theme to this dramatic, controversial, entertaining and exciting book. It is the story of a father and his daughter, who had a wonderful streak of adventures together, through his many marriages, through his decades of substance abuse, show business glory, tabloid headlines, and the untimely ravages of Alzheimer's disease.

On these pages Debby Campbell tells her story of a father and his beloved daughter, written from her heart and from her personal journals. She shares details of the most rewarding years in her father's life, and now for the first time, she blows the lid off of several of Glen Campbell's family secrets. It is about a family bound together by Glen's talent, and ultimately torn apart in conflict. In this frank and touching family memoir Debby Campbell sets the record straight about a devoted daughter's love for her talented father, with the full knowledge that she is about to start burning some very significant bridges of her own.

Ghost On The Canvas

MY name is Debby Campbell. Although I am not a household name, I have been seen onstage, and I have been heard singing in front of countless hundreds of thousands of concert goers and country music fans. For 24 years I was a featured performer in my father's concert show as a singer and as his duet partner. My father is Glen Campbell, and he has had a long career as one of the biggest and most successful singers, television stars, guitar players, and country music stars of the last 50 years. Although I am his oldest child, my relationship with him has been somewhat on-and-off throughout my entire life.

As a singer and performer, I never sought personal fame or notoriety for myself. Certainly, my father had enough fame for both of us. Several of dad's greatest recorded hits were duets with female singing partners including Bobbie Gentry, Anne Murray, Rita Coolidge and Tanya Tucker. Since these ladies couldn't tour with him regularly, in dad's concert show I would be his duet singing partner. It was a wonderful gig, and it brought my dad and I closer together as daughter and father, and as best friends.

Some of my fondest memories are of the adventures I have had with dad. As part of my father's concert show I had the privilege to count John Wayne as a personal friend. The stars of TV's *Bonanza* – Lorne Green and Michael Landon – once came to a party at my dad's house when I was a teenager, and at the time I thought that was absolutely "the ultimate"! I got to share the stage with Andy Williams, the Judds, Trisha Yearwood, Merle Haggard, the Osmond Brothers and John Denver, and to meet show business stars like Burt Reynolds, Loretta Lynn and Gene Autry. I was also there to watch dad give a young hopeful country singer/song-writer by the name of Alan Jackson his first break in show business.

I have gotten to be a part of so many magical moments in my dad's life. Still, these experiences never gave me any personal ambitions to launch my own professional solo singing career. I certainly can sing – I come by that naturally, thanks to dad – but I never longed to become a headliner on my own. There was only one role that I really wanted: that was to be my father's daughter, and to be there for him if he needed me. Accomplishing this goal is something that hasn't always been easy.

While I was in the show, I was treated as his "co-star", which I found very gratifying. I never asked to be billed as: "Glen Campbell, with Special Guest: Debby Campbell", but one day it just appeared on the posters and the advertising, and that's how it was from then onward. Occasionally I even appeared on some of his albums as well.

Yes, I often shared in the glory of dad's life both onstage and offstage. However, I also got to see dad's dark side as well: the substance abuse, the alcohol binges, and some of the wild behavior. I remember going to a taping of the *Midnight Special* TV show with him in the seventies when I was a teenager. While dad was rehearsing onstage, I was backstage waiting for him to return. TV studios are routinely kept at low temperatures because of the hot spotlights. I was really cold backstage, so I put his jacket on. When dad came back from rehearsing and he saw that I was wearing his jacket, he totally freaked out! He quickly asked for his jacket back and said he would find me another one to wear. By then it was too late. I had already put my hand into the outside pocket of the jacket, and I innocently found his vial full of cocaine. I may only have been a naïve teenager, but I knew what I had discovered, and by the look in my eyes he knew that I knew what it was as well. I calmly told him, "What I had found in your outside pocket is now safely in the inside breast pocket of the jacket."

Drugs ran rampant and freely in Hollywood in those days. In dad's eyes, I was a just a kid, but I knew enough about show business to know what a vial of coke was. I didn't really have any judgmental thoughts about it other than the startling realization that dad was using drugs. After that, I also realized that life with my father could at times be a highly unpredictable series of events. What I didn't know at the time was that it was going to be even more unpredictable than even I could have imagined.

My dad's family life is complicated to say the least. He has had four wives, and he has had children with each of them. As dad's oldest child, I often found myself competing with all of my younger half-brothers and half-sisters. There have been several times that I have felt very close to them, and at other times I have felt completely estranged from them. It was like we were all vying for dad's attention, and this is a dynamic that has never changed.

My mother is Diane Kirk, who was dad's first wife. They were married for four years, from 1955 to 1959, and when their marriage was over my mother was left with extremely bitter feelings towards dad. She felt abandoned by him. However, after the marriage was over I struggled to become a regular fixture in my father's personal life and his stage show became my window of opportunity to accomplish this.

As his oldest child, I never doubted my position in my father's life. One of my prize possessions is an album cover which dad autographed to me with the inscription: "To my Darling Daughter, best friend and singing partner. Love, dad Glen Campbell."

For the 24 years I was on the road with dad, I was a regular performer in his show including during his busiest era of headlining the highly demanding Glen Campbell Goodtime Theater in Branson, Missouri. I would be onstage with dad if he ever lost his place in the show, and I was there for many of dad's greatest achievements, and through some of his greatest disappointments, including his traumatic D.U.I. incident in 2003. However, he was able to put his life back on track, and I was there to support and celebrate his new-found sobriety.

Dad had been playing with the same professional and seasoned touring band for over a decade. He felt comfortable with them, and they grew to become supportive friends whom he could lean on, both onstage and offstage. With the exception of his longtime keyboard player, T. J. Kuenster, they were all fired and replaced with Glen's children by his fourth wife, Kim, and their band: Instant People.

Over the next year, dad began to get disoriented, and he seemed more forgetful than he had ever been. It started with a missing lyric onstage, or losing his place in the show, but I was always there – onstage with him – to cover for him. In June 2011, it was officially disclosed to the world that dad was suffering from the early stages of Alzheimer's disease.

Since that time came the release of dad's highly publicized 2011 album, *Ghost On The Canvas*, which features songs and contributions from several young musicians who worship dad's music, including Jakob Dylan, Billy

Corgan of the Smashing Pumpkins, and Chris Isaak. Next came the booking of an elaborate final concert tour for dad.

What I had been witnessing were gradual changes in my father's life, one step at a time. I should have seen it coming, but I didn't. Not until September 18, 2011, when I was swiftly fired from dad's show by his business manager Stan Schneider.

I could see the future of what my relationship with my father was about to become. And, I feared, it will not be for the better. However, before my relationship with dad and his children and my stepmother all becomes an ugly family feud, I want to recount many of my happy memories with my father, who – like a ghost on a canvas – has wandered in and out of my presence throughout my entire life.

This book is not a show-business saga so much as it is a story about a daughter trying to find her way into her father's life through his many trials, tribulations and marriages. Although my father is most well-known for songs like 'By The Time I Get To Phoenix', 'Galveston' and 'Rhinestone Cowboy', for me, the most significant song in his career is his 1966 country hit 'Burning Bridges'. It is a song and a phrase that has meant a lot to me. 'Burning Bridges' was the very first song I professionally sang onstage with my dad, at the Arizona State Fair in 1987.

Ironically enough, when I was fired from my father's band by his business manager, the last two words that Stan said to me were, "Debby, don't '*burn bridges*'."

So if anyone wonders why I wrote this book, it is because a gigantic bridge has been burned out from under me. On these pages is an incredible story of how I stayed in my dad's life against all odds, and how I loved him no matter what the cost. No one can ever take away the memories we shared.

It seems that several of the people around me want to light a match and torch the delicate bridge that I have built to my father's heart. But I won't let them. No matter what happens, I know who I am, and where I fit into his life. This is *Burning Bridges*, I am his daughter and this is my story.

CHAPTER ONE

Mom And Dad

MY dad, Glen Travis Campbell, is originally from Billstown in Pike County, near Billstown, Arkansas. It is rural farming country, and at the time of his birth, on April 22, 1936, the county's population was less than 100 residents. Dad's family accounted for almost one in eight of those residents. He was one of 12 children, born to a sharecropper father of Scottish descent.

My grandfather Wes Campbell's relatives were originally from Scotland, then they moved to Ireland, and from there they came over to America. I recently did some investigating in Salt Lake City, Utah, where I went through a bunch of genealogy records, and I discovered a lot of information about my dad's family. I found Henry Campbell, and I also found dad listed there, Grandpa Wes, Dan, Jesse, and then back to Henry. I was able to trace five generations, all the way back to Ireland.

I went through all of the books listing all of the ships that came into Ellis Island, and there was only one Henry Campbell. I found the ship's manifest, and it listed all of the people who boarded that particular ship. I found that when Henry came over to the United States in the 1800s he was only 18 years old, so it fits into everything that I knew.

My grandfather Wes was married once before he married my Grandma Carrie, and he had two boys by his first marriage: Wayne and Lindell. Then he married my grandma, and together they had 10 children, including two sets of twins. Each of those kids had a lot of children of their own, so there are just a lot of Campbells running around in Billstown, Arkansas.

I have been to Billstown, and it is very small. When dad was living there the population was 311. It is literally a "don't close your eyes, or blink, or you'll miss it" kind of town, or a "you'd have to be going there to get there" type of place. There are two general stores there. All of the houses are small and really spread apart. As dad always says, "We lived so far out in the woods that nobody lived behind us." Some of the most memorable years in my life came from spending time in Arkansas with my grandparents, aunts, uncles, and cousins.

My dad's parents were both very down-to-earth people, like all the Campbells. They were just awesome, and I have so many fond memories of them. I got along great with them, and they were very much loved by everyone they met. They both lived into their eighties.

Dad knew from an early age that he had a love of music, and it was his Uncle Boo who originally taught him how to play the guitar. Young Glen Campbell immediately showed an instinctive talent for playing the instrument, and everyone in the family was aware of it. When he was a teenager, he went to Albuquerque, New Mexico, to live with his Uncle Dick Bills, who was married to dad's Aunt Judy. Dick Bills was a professional musician at the time, so the opportunity of moving west to live with Uncle Dick and Aunt Judy seemed like a great way for dad to break into the music business world.

If this opportunity hadn't come along when it did, who knows if dad would have ever gotten the opportunity to leave Billstown, or a chance to pursue his career in music?

When he moved to Albuquerque, dad immediately found himself playing guitar in his uncle's established band: Dick Bills & The Sandia Mountain Boys. Not only did Dick Bills & The Sandia Mountain Boys perform at two local bars called the Hitching Post and the Chesterfield Club, but Uncle Dick also had a local radio show, and dad would appear on the radio program as well. For him it was an instant introduction to show business, and a golden opportunity for an 18-year-old boy.

It was in Albuquerque that my mother and father first met. My mom's maiden name was Diane Kirk, and she was to become my dad's first wife.

My maternal grandparents were Lucille and John Kirk. My grandfather we called "Dude" or "Grandpa Dude". He had the first Indian trading post in New Mexico, which he owned with his siblings, the Kirk Brothers. He would trade things with the Indians, and he would sell hand-woven Indian blankets, pottery and jewelry to the public. I still have an authentic Indian blanket that my mother gave me that has "Kirk Brothers" on it.

In fact, my grandfather's trading post was written up in the book *Route 66: The Romance Of The West*. That book is all about trading posts and other interesting spots along historic Route 66, and the Kirk Brothers Trading Post is in there. It was located in Gallup, New Mexico.

My grandmother Lucille was a homemaker, and I have wonderful memories of her. I also have some absolutely gorgeous photos of her as a young girl. She was definitely model material, and she was just a stunning looking woman. I just loved her.

My mother was one of seven children. There was John, Tommy, Jody, Venita, Diane, Jimmy, and Vinnie.

The Chesterfield Club was a popular nightclub in Albuquerque. My grandma and grandpa used to go there quite frequently to dance. My mom had seen my dad on *The Dick Bills Noontime Hour* and had mentioned it one day to my grandma. She said, "Isn't he handsome?"

Of course my grandma said, "Well they sometimes play at The Chesterfield Club. So one night we will take you and your sister Venita."

Now, even though the club was a 'nightclub' per se, I guess it was OK to take your kids there, as long as you were with your parents. It wasn't an actual restaurant, but they did serve some food also. So of course mom went, and dad saw her and asked her to dance.

According to my mom, he actually said, "Can I borrow your frame for this dance?" How is that for a funny expression?

Had it not been for the Chesterfield Club I might have not come along. As they say in the movies, "That's where Glen met Diane." At that time my mom was just 15 years old, and dad was 18. After that night they immediately started dating and went together for a year before breaking up. After a couple of months went by, my mom came home from school one day, and found my dad waiting for her.

They got back together, and a few months after that my mom got pregnant. At that time she was just a young girl in the tenth grade in high school. My grandmother Lucille was not happy with this to say the least, especially since her daughter was just a young girl of 16.

According to what mom told me, she and dad were married in a civil ceremony at the court house in Albuquerque. It was my grandfather – along with another witness – who was there with them. My grandmother refused to sign the marriage license and she would not go with them to the court house, since mom was underage.

When dad and the rest of the band were out on the road, mom would usually stay with the steel guitar player's wife, as she was pregnant and 16, and too young to be alone. One night when she was seven months pregnant, she suddenly experienced severe labor pains and I believe mom said it was Marcie – the steel guitar player's wife – who took her to the hospital.

My grandfather went to the hospital and waited with mom while my little brother was born. He was born two months premature, and his lungs weren't fully developed. And of course back in those days they didn't have the technology they do today, to deal with those situations.

My grandparents would not let mom see the baby at all. They thought it would be too traumatic for a 16-year-old to see him, and for him to die in front of her. My brother had no real chance for survival.

Mom was at my grandparents at the time when the hospital call came in, announcing that the baby had died. My dad did not want to go to the hospital with my grandfather, and they got into a huge quarrel. Dad was apparently so mad, that he and my mom just left upset, and they went back to where they lived to grieve over this sad situation.

Although the baby died, and my mom never got to see him, she named him Glen Travis Campbell Jr. How sad it is to think that she never laid her eyes on the baby who would have been my older brother. He died within two weeks of his birth.

I had never heard the details about this whole story before, until recently. It was something that my mother had never spoken of in all of these years. Mom had tears in her eyes as she recounted all of this to me.

Maybe I would have had an older brother if they had known how to deal with premature births back then. This all took place in 1955. I was born a while later in 1956.

There are a couple of photos of my dad and me from back then. In photographs he was so young and handsome it is easy to see why mom fell in love with him.

I once asked mom, "Do you have any photographs of you and dad together when you were married?"

She said to me, "No. We really didn't take a lot of pictures back then." To this day, I hardly have any pictures of my mom, so I can surely attest to that fact. According to her, she never has needed photos to remind her of her life and where she has been.

Mom told me that in addition to the Chesterfield Club, she also went to the Hitching Post as well, just to watch dad play after they were married. She also said that dad wouldn't let her dance with anyone other than the band members during the band's intermission.

She also told me that grandma used to make the shirts for the band. I do remember my grandma being quite the seamstress.

Personally, I remember nothing about any events from that era when my dad and my mom were together. I can look at what few photographs exist from those years back in Albuquerque to give me a vision of that time, but I was still too young to remember very much really specific from the fifties.

Mom and dad's marriage didn't last a long time at all. In fact, they decided to get divorced after just four years. Considering the duration of most teen marriages, they actually had quite a long relationship for kids that young. They basically decided that it wasn't going to last in the long run, so they started out with a "trial separation" of a year.

According to New Mexico law, a couple had to be separated for an entire year before the state would grant you a divorce. I think that the logic was that you might have a possible reconciliation if you didn't wait for a year. They gave people a 12 month chance to see if their relationship was going to work out or not.

From my perspective, it seemed to me that my mother and father always got along with each other, even though their marriage didn't last. Including the year they dated before they got married, their relationship was one that only went on for five years in total. They were divorced in 1959.

After my mother and father decided to split up, mom went to live with her sister and brother-in-law: my Aunt Venita and Uncle Joe Carmer. Meanwhile, dad met a woman by the name of Billie, and they began a relationship. He had met Billie in Albuquerque as well. By the time I reached my fourth birthday, my mom and dad were already living separate lives.

Even after they split up, they were still friendly with each other. I was talking to mom recently, and she said to me, "There were times when I was living with your aunt and uncle, after the divorce, that your dad still came over and visited us." I think that it would be fair to say that mom was still in love with dad, even though they were divorced.

In spite of any emotional ties that they still had for each other, or feelings that they harbored for each other, I really feel that they would have broken up eventually anyway. They had simply grown apart.

Dad had obviously expressed his show-business career desires to her. Even though he was just a local musician in Albuquerque, he had already told her that he wanted to at least take a shot at the big time, in a big city with more opportunities. If that is all that you want to do, you at least have to strive for the big trophy. Everybody wants to excel at what they do, and if you are playing a guitar, then that's going to eventually have a calling for you somewhere more sophisticated than New Mexico.

Mom was just never made for the kind of life that the wife of a musician has. She just wasn't. It is simply as plain as that.

My mom is someone who is totally without any pretense. She was a very fifties "homemaker" kind of mom. In fact, she was always the perfect homemaker. Mom would have cookies baked when I came home from school, dinner on the table every night, and that kind of simple and idyllic home life.

Mom has also always loved animals. I remember that at my grandmother's home, there were always lots of Siamese cats running around at the house. So, mom was raised loving animals. I think that she grew into being somewhat of a homebody because of this. She could never go anywhere for long periods of time, because there were always pets to take care of, and that was very important to her. She was the type of person who would never go on overnight trips anywhere, because there was always an animal – if not several animals – to take care of at home in the morning.

How could she ever be married to a man who was a musician, who regularly had out-of-town gigs? Her marriage to dad was never going to work out in the long run.

On the other hand, my relationship with my mother was always a close one. Since my mom was only 17 or 18 years old when she had me, we were very close in age. In a way, it was like we grew up together. Throughout my life, she was more like a friend to me than a mom.

Not long after he began his marriage to Billie, dad had already decided to move to Los Angeles. He loved to play the guitar, and there was only so far that he could go with a career in music in Albuquerque, so he decided that he had to move west to California if he was ever going to have a real shot at pursuing his dreams. Unlike my mother, Billie loved that idea.

My dad was always very different from my mom. In fact, they were exact opposites. Mom wanted to stay at home and take care of me, tend to the house, and care for her pets. Dad had a taste of what the life of a successful touring musician could be, and he longed for more. Dad always delighted in having the spotlight. He loved being onstage with other musicians, and he always felt happy and confident in a group setting as a musician having a great time making music and entertaining people along with his friends.

Looking back on this era, I truly feel that my parents would have divorced eventually, especially after dad became a big name in the music business, and in the whole show-business world. He was a talented and handsome young man who at least wanted to have his shot at the big time. Mom, on the other hand, isn't someone who could have, or would have, gotten into the dynamics of the music scene – let alone the Hollywood fast lane. That simply is not her lifestyle at all. They both had their own dream of what their lives should be like. Unfortunately, they were dreaming totally different dreams.

CHAPTER TWO

A Child Of Divorce

IN 1960, dad and Billie left Albuquerque and moved to Los Angeles, and mom and I stayed in New Mexico. It was the beginning of a different kind of relationship for dad and me. Often it was a long distance relationship.

After my mom and dad split up, for a couple of years I remained in Albuquerque with mom. Eventually my mom remarried to a man named Danny Reed. That marriage was short-lived, because I don't really have any memories of Danny at all. Billie and dad would later tell me stories about when they would come to get me, or drop me off, Danny would supposedly hold them off by pretending he had a shotgun. I did ask my mom about this recently, and she said, "He never had a gun," but that he was not keen on dad.

Together mom and Danny had a daughter, my half-sister Donna. Not long afterward they divorced.

When my mother got married for the third time it was to an active military man. His name is Jack Moilanen, and he would regularly get transferred from one military base to another. For that reason, the majority of my growing-up years were spent in so many different places. Jack is the only true stepdad that I have ever known, and he and mom are still married to this day.

I became a child of divorce, spending some of my time with my mother and Jack, and spending some of my time with dad and Billie. When I was growing up, I would spend the school year with mom, and most summers were spent in Los Angeles with my dad. There was also a time when Jack was transferred to England, and dad would come over there on tour, so I would get to spend time with him there.

I have fond memories of the holidays with mom and Jack. At Christmas, my stepdad would buy the biggest tree that he could find, and they would flock it with snow. He was very particular about how our Christmas trees looked. They had to be just so perfect, and my stepdad made certain that they were exactly the way he wanted them. He may have been in the military, but he was also very sensitive about things like that. He was very easygoing.

When I lived with my mom and my stepdad, we always had one pet or another. When I was growing up, I remember that I had Suzy, who was a black Labrador retriever. It also wasn't long before mom and Jack had a daughter, Denise. I grew up with both of my half-sisters, Donna and Denise.

Meanwhile, dad and Billie started a family of their own. It wasn't long before I had two half-brothers – Travis and Kane – and a half-sister – Kelli. And so, my already complicated family tree began to grow.

My school years were spent all over the map. I was in first grade to fifth grade in Roswell, New Mexico; and during sixth grade we were living in L'Anse, in the upper peninsula of Michigan. That was because my stepdad went to Vietnam, and that was where his family was from: L'Anse, Michigan. L'Anse is right on the shores of Lake Superior, where it is very cold in the winter. When I was in the seventh, eighth, ninth, and half of tenth grade, we lived in Clovis, New Mexico.

In 1968, at the height of dad's fame, with his initial hit records, a growing list of Grammy Awards, and his own weekly network television program, he was a big Hollywood star. That year *Photoplay* magazine sent a reporter to New Mexico to track mom down, to interview her for an article called, "Glen Campbell's First Marriage Helped His Second Marriage". The reporter also interviewed my Aunt Venita and the owner of a local club where dad used to play with his Uncle Dick Bills.

Mom was quoted as saying, "I remember all too well the happy days we had. We had many many wonderful times together. When Debbie was born, why it seemed to me as though Glen must have been the happiest man in the world. It's true that in the last few months of the marriage neither of us was happy. Somehow we had grown apart."

Citing the reason that their marriage did not work, mom explained at the time, "I'm just an old homebody. Which wasn't too good, I guess, this wanting to stay at home all the time." She also proclaimed, "I'm awfully happy now. I've got a good man and we've made a good life."

When mom's sister – my Aunt Venita – was interviewed by the *Photoplay* reporter she was asked about mom's marriage to my dad. She explained, "It's over, it's been over for a long, long time. Both Glen and Diane have had their hurts from it, but each has found a new happiness. It's funny. If Glen hadn't become such a big success no one would ever think about it any more."

At the time, dad was a huge internationally recognized success with his concurrent CBS-TV show *The Glen Campbell Goodtime Hour* on every Wednesday at 7:30 p.m., and hits on both sides of the Atlantic. Recalling his catapulting his way to stardom, Aunt Venita claimed, "Glen was soon living in another world. The music, the excitement, the applause, the admiration from so many people. It was what he wanted and he worked hard to get it."

Then came the topic of me! At the time I was spelling my name "Debbie". According to the *Photoplay* article, mom said, "Debbie is a very sensitive little girl. She loves to hear from Glen. Hardly a day goes by that she doesn't come home from school and ask, 'Have I got a letter, Mama?' When she doesn't hear from him she takes it hard. She's the spitting image of Glen and she just idolizes him. Last month when she was on the local talent show and sang Glen's song, 'By The Time I Get To Phoenix', I went and saw it and just about bawled. I said, 'I wished Glen could have been there to play guitar behind her.' She's going to be in the show again in a few weeks, at the auditorium. Debbie keeps asking me if Glen could come and see her. It's hard to tell her that it's something I couldn't ask Glen to do. This time Debbie's going to sing 'Wichita Lineman'. She has a pretty voice and I think she could do well. But that is something Glen will have to decide, though I hope for Debbie's sake, that he approves. Her heart is so set on it."

Meanwhile, my stepfather, Jack, continued to work for the military, and he was constantly transferred from one place to the next. After our second stint in New Mexico, Jack was transferred to Europe, and across the Atlantic Ocean we went.

When we moved to Lakenheath, England, I would see dad when he would come to England to do shows. He would send a limo to pick me up at the Air Force base, which was a few hours away from London. I was always so embarrassed when it would arrive, as everyone would be looking out their windows, wondering what was going on, and trying to figure out how I rated a limousine.

Part of the excitement and fun was getting to see Barry, who was usually the limousine driver. One year when Barry came to get me, he arrived with a huge surprise for me in the trunk of his limousine. He knew that I loved Diana Ross and her music. He had recently driven a limousine for her in England, and he had gotten a lot of stuff for me from Diana Ross. I was so thrilled. I wonder where Barry is today? He is someone I would love to locate, and see again. What a sweet guy he was!

Sometimes dad would let me bring one of my friends along with me to London, so that I would have someone to pal around with while he was busy doing interviews and such.

I also always enjoyed spending time with Roger Adams, who was dad's agent. Roger was always so nice to me as well. When dad was in London Roger was always there with him, and sometimes Roger's lovely wife Joanne would accompany him. What a great family Roger had. And later on when I started singing with dad, Roger was also traveling with us. He and dad and I spent a lot of time together in hotel rooms watching *Wheel Of Fortune* on TV and betting quarters on who could guess the puzzle first. When we were in Australia, Roger bought his daughter Bridget a ring and dad bought me one too.

When Roger passed away, I went to his memorial in Santa Fe, New Mexico, with dad and Kim. His wife Joanne later sent me a box with all the memorabilia that Roger had collected over the years, as well as his beautiful Burberry coat that I always loved to see Roger wearing. He always looked liked a *proper* Englishman in it.

I remember that the big "hang-out" spot in London in those days was the Playboy Club. England often lived up to its reputation for bland cuisine, and the Playboy Club was the only place in town where you could get a decent American-style hamburger. They were really good!

One year we were in England with Tom and Dick Smothers. I still have a picture from that time. And another year I remember being there with Burt Reynolds and the Harlem Globetrotters. I was around 15 or 16 at that time, and dad was doing some BBC-TV specials.

Without a doubt, one of the most memorable things that happened in those days was meeting and getting to know dad's *True Grit* co-star, John Wayne. He was absolutely wonderful, and so genuinely nice to me. I will never forget sitting and carrying on a conversation with "The Duke", as he was known. That was very special to me. He even sent me a photo of himself that was autographed: "Debby, my friend when are you coming to see me again? John Wayne."

The ironic thing was that I actually got to see dad a lot more while living in England than I did most years when I lived in the United States. There were less distractions for him in England, and I was his only child in England during those visits.

All of us have certainly had our share of crushes on teen idols, or movie stars, or athletes, or musical performers whose posters we had taped or hung up on our bedroom walls. As a teenager, the music I always listened to was mainly soul music. I loved the music of Motown, the Stylistics, the Chi-lites, Barry White, and all of that kind of music. My favorite female singers were Diana Ross and Barbra Streisand. I have all the Streisand movies. For male singers, my all-time favorite guys were Elvis Presley and Neil Diamond.

However, when I was a teenager, my own father was a handsome and publicly recognized TV star as well. He had huge number one hit records, and he was also a movie star. Yet for me, it was beyond my realm to think that my own father could be the romantic dream of other teenagers. At the time, I never once thought of dad as being anything else but "my dad."

In my mind, he was the guy who told me to clean my room, or told me how late I could stay up at night. I could never have seen him from any other perspective. However, it did create some strange moments when we were out in public together.

When I was living in England, and 16 or 17 years old, dad was a very recognizable star. British audiences have always loved him. Dad was often in London for concert tours or to promote his latest albums. On one such occasion, I had gone with him when he was giving some sort of radio press interview, and a group of his most devoted fans had gotten word that he was there in the studio "in the flesh". I remember it as if it was yesterday. Dad had just finished the interview, and we were leaving the radio station. I was just getting in the car, and dad was standing outside of the car, when all of a sudden a mob of screaming female fans were rapidly coming towards us at an alarming pace. It was like a feeding frenzy of teenage girls! I had never seen anything like this before, and it instantly scared me to death.

One of the few photos taken of my dad and myself in the 1950s in New Mexico, where I was born. Dad was so young and handsome it is easy to see why mum fell in love with him.

Dad and me in New Mexico, around 1957 or 1958. Because they divorced when I was just three years old I don't remember much about life with my dad and mom together.

In the summers I would go to Hollywood to stay with dad and his second wife, my stepmother Billie. She always treated me like I was one of her own kids. Here I am (left) with Billie and my half siblings Kelli, Travis, and Kane Campbell.

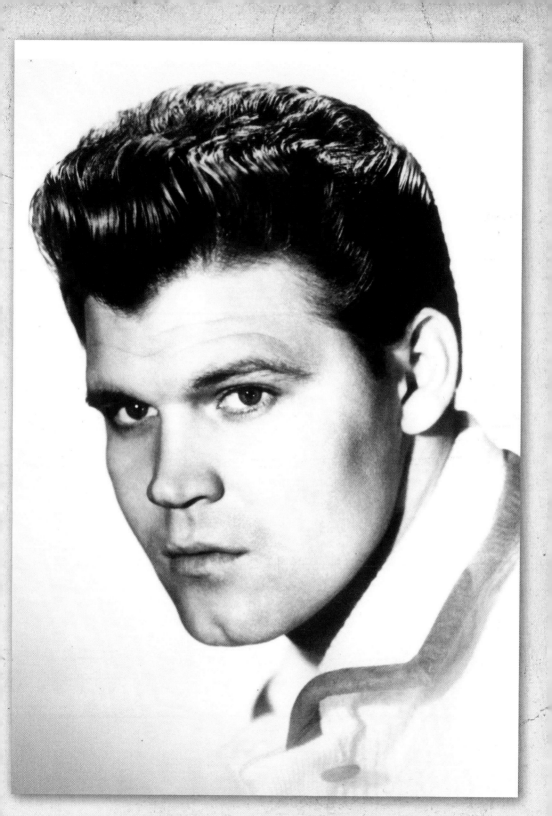

Dad moved from New Mexico to Los Angeles in 1960 to pursue a career in the music business. He started out as the guitar player in the studio group known as The Wrecking Crew. His guitar playing was heard on hit records by Elvis Presley, Frank Sinatra, Dean Martin, The Monkees, The Mamas & The Papas, The Beach Boys and Sonny & Cher.

I would see dad whenever he was doing concert tours in England, since I lived there at the time. Left to right: my school friend Felicia, Tom Smothers, me, Dick Smothers, Joe Somaruga and dad.

Dad showing off his bagpipe playing skills with The Royal Scots Guards, in Las Vegas in the 1960s. England, Scotland, Ireland and Wales were among dad's favorite places to tour. His many fans there have loved him since the beginning of his career.

His success on the CBS-TV show *The Glen Campbell Goodtime Hour* led to dad becoming a huge television star. Here he is on a 1969 episode of his show, singing with Neil Diamond, and Cher – whose early records often featured dad on guitar.

With my friend Felicia, Burt Reynolds and my dad on the set of his 1974 TV special, *Glen Campbell The Musical West*, which was filmed in England. This was from the same show that also starred John Wayne, Burl Ives and Michelle Lee. I always loved watching my dad work on his shows and his music.

Although music fans the world over knew my dad as a handsome, guitar-playing singer, TV and movie star, to me he was always just one thing: my dad. Throughout all of his four marriages, and his several moves around the country, he actively remained an important part of my life.

My dad on stage during a proud moment with his parents, my grandparents: Carrie and Wes Campbell. This cherished photo hangs on the wall of my house in Arizona.

My friend Cindy Biggs and me with my dad in London while I was at school there. At the time dad and Billie lived in the Hollywood house that I refer to as "the mansion".

To My Darling Daughter Love you more than life Dad

I have such wonderful memories of John Wayne and dad around the time they made the hit film *True Grit*. John Wayne was a wonderful man and I cherished his friendship.

This is "the mansion" that Billie built. It was so huge that I was actually intimidated to move into it. Coming from a little house on an Air Force base and moving to a huge eight-bedroom house was a bit surreal for me.

I grabbed dad and literally yanked him into the car, fearing he would have gotten absolutely trampled, if not torn apart by this souvenir-hungry mob of young women. We slammed and locked the doors, and as the car pulled away, I thought we had escaped being attacked by an out-of-control mob.

"God dad, they would have ripped your clothes off of you if I hadn't dragged you into this car!" I exclaimed with concern.

"I've seen it get worse than this!" he said, just laughing it off. Obviously, he had been in situations like this before, and he had been the subject of this kind of crazy behavior in the past.

For me, it was really an eye-opening experience. I had never witnessed a situation where I had feared for my own safety at the hands of a throng of over-enthusiastic teenagers.

"They would have torn you apart for souvenirs!" I proclaimed.

I looked over to dad, and he just smiled and shook his head. Although he was a little annoyed by the craziness of the whole situation, deep down inside I'm sure he was quite flattered by it.

Although I witnessed scenes like this that my dad's presence incited, it was still impossible for me to think of the public's perspective on "Glen Campbell" being anything more than just my father.

I do recall people saying to me, "Oh, my God, I had your dad's poster on my bedroom wall." It always put me in a state of shock to hear such a pronouncement.

If anyone said anything like that to me, I would just plug my ears, and started singing, "Nah, nah, nah-nah, nah nah nah . . ." to block their words out. On more than one occasion I've had to announce, "I don't want to know that you have a sex crush on my father!"

I made certain that I kind of laughingly played it off. Since I can't think of him as anything more than "dad", I didn't even want to hear about it – let alone be forced to envision it!

While living in England with my mom and stepfather, I finished high school and graduated in 1974. My stepfather, Jack, still had two more years during which he was going to be stationed in England, and since I was not a British citizen, I couldn't work there, so I decided to head back to the United States. It was in early 1975 that I flew to Los Angeles and moved in with dad and Billie in "the big house" in the Hollywood Hills.

During this era, dad's recording career was hotter than ever. He had huge number one hits on the charts with 'Rhinestone Cowboy' (1975), 'Country Boy (You Got Your Feet in L.A.)' (1975), 'Don't Pull Your Love'/'Then You Can Tell Me Goodbye' (1976), 'Sunflower' (1977) and 'Southern Nights' (1977), so he was at a new peak of his career, and he was kept busy recording and touring. It was a highly successful time for him.

Since mom and dad's divorce, dad and Billie had three children of their own: Kelli, Travis and Kane. Kelli is five years younger than me, and she is the oldest of the three. Basically, I was just part of this "one big happy family", who just happened to live in a gigantic mansion.

That was the big house that Billie built. It was really a great house. It was huge, and I was actually intimidated by it when I moved in. Coming from a little house on an Air Force base to a huge eight-bedroom house, it was a bit surreal. Somebody could have lived there for a month, and you would have never known they were there, it was so huge!

Oh my gosh, it was astonishing. I was just a small town girl, living with my mom and my stepdad on an Air Force base, and suddenly here I was smack-dab in the middle of Los Angeles, in Hollywood no less!

This humongous house on the hill was a fascinating experience to say the least. It was such a maze of rooms that I was scared to go anywhere in the house by myself for the first week for fear that I might get lost. Yet as big as it was, Billie had a knack for making it very homey inside. Every room was comfortably furnished although for the life of me I couldn't understand some of the design choices. I was especially astonished by some of the bright colors that were used. I remember thinking, "Why would anyone put lime green carpeting throughout their bedroom?" Well, there was a very logical reason! It was Billie's favorite color so somehow it made perfect sense.

At dad and Billie's house I didn't have my own room, but I shared a room with my cousin, Jheri Kay – who was my Aunt Billie's daughter – as she was living there at the time as well. She eventually moved out, and then I had that back bedroom all to myself. The house that dad and Billie and their three kids lived in had eight bedrooms, so there was plenty of room for them to have house guests. The house on the hill also had extra bedrooms downstairs for the housekeepers and cooks: Auntie, Dida and Lolita. So, it was nothing short of a mansion, with three distinctively different living areas to it.

Although it was a little daunting to live there, it was the kind of a house that was ideal for giving parties. They would have big Halloween parties, and I remember a big celebration they had where Lorne Greene and Michael Landon – the stars of the TV series *Bonanza* – came. I was so impressed! It was exciting for me, but at the same time it was a bit bizarre. I was so unused to this whole Hollywood scene. The house in itself was overwhelming, and then to top it off – to have some of the biggest stars of the era in the living room – made it seem even more surreal. I was just kind of thrown into the mix of all of this.

Country singing star Roger Miller used to come to the house all the time, since he and dad were such great friends. Another talented man who was often at the house was Jerry Fuller, who wrote the Ricky Nelson hit 'Travelin' Man', with his wife Annette. I have so many great memories of those days!

Suddenly finding myself living in Los Angeles was such a huge change for me after my modest small-town Air Force base life. Of course Kelli and Travis had friends who were the children of people in the business, as that is the only life they had ever known. Kelli was great friends with actor and teen idol Leif Garrett. I didn't quite know how to handle all of this. For me it was culture shock.

I didn't know how to be around those people. I just didn't know how to relate to the children of TV stars. To find my footing in this bizarre new world that I found myself in the middle of, I cultivated a much different circle of friends. While Kelli was friends with the children of media stars, I found myself hanging out with people who were down on their luck, down-to-earth, or who had little money at all.

I also spent a lot of my time with dad and Billie's housekeepers, Auntie and Dida. They were so nice and friendly towards me, and they had absolutely no pretense at all. That was more within my comfort zone. Auntie and Dida would take me to some of their family functions where they would cook a pig in the ground. They were from the Philippines and to this day I still have a strong love of Filipino food.

In spite of all of this, I fit right into the family when I went to stay with dad and Billie. My half-sister Kelli and I acted like typical kids, and we would fight with each other. You know how sisters will argue with each other. Kelli and I were always like typically competitive sisters, and "sibling rivalry" was definitely at play.

Often we would fight about dad. My standard retort during my arguments with her would often end with me insisting, "Well, he was *my* dad first!" That being said, I always got along great with all of them.

I remember when they lived off of Laurel Canyon Drive on Allenwood from my summers when I had come to visit in the past. They had a nice sized house there. Then they later built this absolutely huge mansion of a house on Edwin in Laurel Canyon. This new place dwarfed the one they previously lived in.

I have such great memories of those days as a teenager in Hollywood. I also have fond memories of T.K., who was Billie and dad's dog. He was named T.K. because those were Travis and Kelli's initials.

Billie Jean was my first stepmom and she warmly welcomed me into their home for all the years they were married. I don't recall having any ill feelings of being left out. Whenever I was there, I was just "one of the family".

One of the first things I had to do in order to live in Los Angeles was to learn to drive a car. You can't get anywhere in L.A. without a car, so Billie put me in driver's school, and I got a California driver's license and a car. I distinctly remember my first car, because I thought it was the most awesome automobile on the planet! It was a purple Chevy Vega, and it was the station-wagon version of that car. I was so proud of that Vega, and I was so excited to show it off to everybody. With my own car I was able to get a job and get around town.

I am someone who always wanted to work for a living, and I thought it would be great fun to work in dad's office. So off to work I went. I had so much fun. I worked with his manager Stan's daughter Andrea there also, and we became great friends. We had a great time together. Rosemary was dad's secretary at the time. I would handle all of dad's fan mail that he received from all over the world. My job would entail sending out pictures and such to all who requested them and sending out the regular newsletters. Little did I know that I would also be doing these things for dad's fans some years later.

While working in his office I also ordered things that dad wanted so it was really a fun job to have. Dad had an album jukebox in the house so he would sometimes have me order certain albums from the record companies, and they were always willing to oblige. And they at most always would send "doubles" so I still have several unopened first edition copies of vinyl albums such as Grand Funk Railroad, Yes and many more from back then.

I don't recall exactly what happened, but the job eventually came to an end. Rosemary ended up leaving. But that was my first job living in Los Angeles and it was a very exciting one to say the least.

I don't remember Billie from Albuquerque, prior to her and dad moving to California. However, over the years she had become one of the key figures in my life of "juggling families". Although I would live most of my time with mom and Jack in their various homes, every year I had the opportunity to go and spend several weeks of my summer vacation in Los Angeles, so over the years, Billie and I became very close.

I always loved Billie, and she was just great towards me. Although I had my younger siblings – Travis, Kane, and Kelli – there too, from the very start, Billie always treated me like one of her kids. I had been just a young girl at the time that she married dad, and she generously let me come into her life at that point. I never thought of her as "the evil stepmom", like the ones some children of divorce may have. Billie always treated me wonderfully, and she always made me feel like I belonged wherever we were, or whatever we were doing.

I can honestly say that I don't really have any bad memories of trying to fit into the family with Kelli, Travis and Kane. As long as I was there, I felt like that was where I belonged.

I would also go along with Billie to visit her mom and dad in Carlsbad, New Mexico, when they made trips there. I felt like a part of all of their lives. I remember her parents Lily and Frank Nunley, and her siblings: Pete, who was Billie's sister, and her brother Pat.

Although I was living in Los Angeles so I could spend time with dad, I would mostly be visiting Billie and the kids since dad did a lot of touring during the summer. But sometimes we would all go on those tours with him. I remember staying at the Ilikai Hotel in Hawaii on one of those tours. I also recall staying at a house in Hawaii, where country singer Jerry Reed and several other performers were around also. I remember those adventures as very happy times for me.

Like any typical teenager in Los Angeles soon I had my own circle of friends, and we would hang out at the Starwood nightclub. Located on the northwest corner of Santa Monica Boulevard and Crescent Heights Avenue in West Hollywood, the Starwood was quite a happening scene.

It was a place where rock groups like the Go-Go's, the Ramones, the Runaways, and Van Halen all played before they became big.

Another place that I ran around was at the Roxy on Sunset Boulevard. I am still in contact with a lot of the kids I met back then. Maureen Kelly was one of the friends I used to hang out with. Although Maureen is no longer with us – may she rest in peace – her daughter is well known actress Minka Kelly, whom I have never met.

For me, the mid-seventies in Hollywood was such a crazy whirlwind time of drugs and alcohol, and all of the fun stuff that teenagers could get into back then. I was 18 years old at the time, so I was having a blast being unleashed in the whole teenage Hollywood scene that was happening at the time.

Dad and Anne Murray recorded a very popular duet album in the early seventies and she had been a regular performer on several seasons of *The Glen Campbell Goodtime Hour*. At one point I went on tour with dad and Anne in Europe and she had this amazing cape that I absolutely fell in love with, so dad had the designer of it – Manuel – make one for me. Manuel was the head designer and tailor who worked for the iconic country designer known as "Nudie". Nudie created outfits for all of the country stars and for rock stars too. I actually still have my cape to this day.

I had some funny adventures with dad back in those days. Several times I would find myself in some sort of public place, like a store, and these totally bizarre incidents would occur. On one occasion, I was in Los Angeles with dad, and he had just had a "perm" put in his hair, to make it really curly.

He had gone over to Japan to do a photo shoot for a commercial. As I recall, it was for Coca-Cola, and they had put this perm in his hair for that, to give it more body. I still have this sticker somewhere that was from that Coke campaign. Dad always used to wear these little tams – these hats – with his sunglasses, and with this perm in his hair his little curls would hang out from underneath it.

We were in a Los Angeles grocery store together one day, and some woman came up to dad and said, "Oh my God I love you! I can't believe you're here! I'm so excited to see you."

Dad smiled to accept the obvious compliment from the star-struck woman.

However, as she continued to speak she gushed out, "I never thought I would run into John Davidson in the grocery store!"

Dad's eyes popped open to hear this, and I stood there with a dumb-founded look on my face.

"I'm Glen Campbell," dad said in a sober tone of voice.

She obviously knew and recognized dad's face, but she didn't even know John Davidson from Glen Campbell. Somehow she couldn't keep her singing TV stars straight in her own mind!

After she walked away I just laughed out loud. "Oh my God!" I said, "She thought you were John Davidson! How did she mistake you for him?"

Dad just rolled his eyes. Clearly he was not flattered by this case of mistaken identity. I however, thought it was totally amusing!

Everyone who is in show business longs to be recognized as a huge star. Imagine the irony of being publicly recognized as a famous TV star – only the wrong one!

The funny thing was that John Davidson didn't have curly hair either. Both he and dad were known for their big, thick blond bouffants of straight hair. I don't know where this woman was coming from. And I certainly have no idea how she mistook dad for John Davidson, especially with his hair with a perm in it, but she certainly did. I teased dad about that for weeks.

This was just another episode that reinforced my belief that there are parts of the show-business realm which are totally insane. It is as if people are drawn to the idea of "fame" like it is some sort of magical commodity. There were times like these when I witnessed the fact that some people can't even get a celebrity's name right, but they are obviously so impressed with the idea of fame itself that they lose their entire sense of reality about it. It also made me wonder, "What does John Davidson do when he is mistaken for Glen Campbell?!"

Another place that I went with dad was Las Vegas. I remember ending up at the Teen Club at the Las Vegas Hilton Hotel when I was a kid, and dad was performing there. Since I was too young to be admitted in the casino or the bars, this would be where I would hang out when he did his shows. It was like an alcohol-free daycare center for teenagers.

When dad was booked at the Riviera Hotel for weeks at a time, I found myself making a lot of friends there. I made friends with a woman named Annie who owned the beauty shop at the Riviera as well as the Stardust. She had a son my age so she would invite me to go water skiing with them all the time at Lake Mead. She became like a mom to me when I was staying there.

Many years later I would end up renting her house in Las Vegas – that I used to stay in – when I moved from Branson, before finally settling back in Arizona. We are still friends, and I saw her when she came to dad's concert at the Hilton Hotel in June 2012.

Unfortunately, things change and not long after my move to Los Angeles was the beginning of the end of dad and Billie's marriage. It was a very bitter divorce, and I really don't know why it happened.

I don't remember them ever having fights, or dramatic conflicts with each other in the house; it all just seemed to suddenly unravel. When their break-up happened, Billie got to keep the house, dad moved out, and I was told that I had to move out too.

To make things even more stressful, I was told by dad and by Stan – who was dad's manager – that because of the divorce I would have to cut all ties with Billie since my loyalty was to my dad and not to her. So how does one do this? Billie was a *major* part of my life for 17 years, as that is how long they were married. And of course I was deeply hurt by this edict.

By now I had grown so close to Billie. She was so genuine and sincere about everything that she did. Kids can recognize true kindness in people, and that is what I had always felt from her. I had felt comfortable around her from the minute I met her. She never made me feel like an outsider in her world, I simply thought that Billie and her three kids were my second family.

I felt this edict was incredibly cruel and unfair. This woman had been in my life for most of my adolescence. So, now for someone to tell me that I can't have anything to do with her anymore really hurt and confused me.

It is one thing for normal kids who have their parents divorce, and they have to come up with a way to have a relationship with both parents. But I had siblings from this marriage. I had Kelli, Travis, and Kane who I felt close to as well. I asked my dad, "How can you tell me I can't have anything to do with Billie when she is their mom, and I have to see them?" But dad laid down the law.

It made for a mess, and it really caused a problem between Billie and me for a while. I remember that dad had brought Kelli and me stereo systems back from Japan after he had been over there doing that Coca-Cola commercial. They were really great top-of-the-line stereo systems. Mine was installed in my bedroom that I lived in at the Hollywood house.

When I was forced to move out and couldn't have anything to do with Billie anymore, she wouldn't let me have my stereo. She must have figured, "Well, since you won't have anything to do with me anymore, then I am not going to give you your stereo!" I remember being so angry and frustrated to be put in this position. It felt terrible. This made me both hurt and confused. I thought her feelings for me had changed because I wasn't her daughter but my dad's.

At first I went and lived with my friends Pascale and Marsha. Then the three of us rented an apartment together, and then I moved into my own apartment at a building in Burbank called the Oakwoods, which dad owned.

My second job was working at a T-shirt shop on Hollywood Boulevard. I also got involved with the Church of Scientology for a brief time. I was hanging around with Larry McNeeley and his wife and they were involved in that church too. I had a lot of L. Ron Hubbard books about Scientology back then that they had given me to read.

After my run of working at the T-shirt place, I took a job at a retirement community. I remember that it was a place where all of the residents were Jewish. It went from 10:00 a.m. until 7:00 p.m. I worked there in the cafeteria, and it was the perfect job for me, since I got off work in time to go and hang out with my friends. And, I didn't have to go in until 10:00 a.m., so I got to sleep in a little bit. So, I did that for a while.

I am the type of person who has always had a job, if not two jobs at once. I have always been working, that is just how I am geared. I always have to be working and paying my own way.

I stayed in Los Angeles for a while longer. It was a whirlwind time. I don't remember a lot of the details as "recreational" drugs had moved into my life and into my dad's life as well.

I remember going to a taping of the TV show *The Midnight Special* with dad during this era. As I recall, it was the episode where Helen Reddy was the host, and I know George Benson was on the show also, along with dad. I can't be sure if it was all the same episode, since I had been to *The Midnight Special* a couple of times with him. However, I do remember meeting the show's producer, Burt Sugarman, at that time too.

I recall going into the dressing room, and standing against the back door, and seeing this woman glaring at me, with an expression on her face like: "Who is this girl in my room?" After dad did his onstage rehearsal with Ms. Reddy, he introduced us. He said, "Helen, this is my daughter Debby."

Suddenly Helen warmed up and said in a friendly tone of voice, "Oh, it is so nice to meet you."

While he was onstage rehearsing, I was really freezing cold in his dressing room backstage, so I put my dad's jacket on. It was just a regular suit jacket, not an overcoat. When he came back from rehearsing onstage and he saw that I had his jacket on, he absolutely freaked out. He quickly asked for his jacket back and he told me that he would find me another one to wear.

Obviously, he was acting paranoid about something. By then it was too late to shield me from the secret he was keeping from me. I had already reached into the pocket of his jacket to keep my hands warm. As I had done so, I had already found his vial of cocaine that was stashed in the outside pocket.

I calmly told him, "Dad, what was in the outside pocket of your jacket is now in the inside pocket." That was all that was said, but in that instant he knew that I knew what was in there. I didn't really have any judgmental thoughts about it at the time, other than the fact that I now knew that my dad was using coke. It was the seventies, and the height of the "me" decade, so drugs ran rampant and freely in Hollywood in those days, and I wasn't that naïve.

It was kind of a moment of revelation for me. I certainly never thought that dad was doing drugs at that time. As I recall, there was so much going on between dad and Billie, and everything else that was happening, that my knowledge that he was doing coke was something of a trivial fact in the larger scenario of what was going on in my life.

Since I was only 17 years old when dad and Billie's marriage totally fell apart, it was truly devastating for me. The most traumatic part of this event was the fact that I was so close with Billie and now she was suddenly missing from my life. In fact she was like a second mother to me.

What really fascinated me was witnessing a whole new side of dad's personality: his ability to suddenly cut people out of his life like they didn't exist anymore. I was shocked by this kind of behavior.

Dad was already off on his next relationship, with the woman who was destined to become his third wife, Sarah Davis. She had been married to Mac Davis at the time that she met dad. The four of them had been friends. Then when Sarah and Mac had marital problems, and dad and Billie had trouble in their marriage as well, everyone was suddenly free and unencumbered. To make a long story short: when Mac and Sarah got a divorce, and dad and Billie split up, dad and Sarah got together. When dad and Sarah started dating, I remember hanging out with her several times when I was with dad. She would come around, and we'd do stuff together.

I liked Sarah and we spent some time together. Dad seemed really happy at the time. Sarah and dad were married in 1977 and things were good for him I guess. I was still in Hollywood, but once he got together with Sarah I didn't see much of him. I had moved to Los Angeles to spend time with dad and Billie, and now I wasn't seeing either of them.

I felt lost at this point. I was forbidden from contacting Billie, so she was out of my life. Then dad threw himself into his new relationship with Sarah, and suddenly he was out of my life as well, although we all lived in the same town.

Ultimately, I made the decision to go against dad's wishes and re-establish my relationship with Billie. When I got back into contact with her I was happy and relieved to find out that she was as warm and welcoming as ever, and I was glad to continue to have her in my life.

However, this soon became complicated as well. Whenever my friends had come to see me, while dad and Billie were married, my friends ended up hanging out with and befriending Billie as well. I had begun to feel that I was being used so that they could have access to Billie. Then when Billie was out of my life – due to dad's edict that I was forbidden to see her – some of my friends continued to visit Billie without me.

Billie was so sweet and warm, and generous to everyone. I again got into the habit of taking my Hollywood friends with me when I would go see her. Unfortunately, some of my friends were so impressed with Billie and her lavish lifestyle that I felt a bit betrayed. My friends were dazzled by the stature of Billie and her mansion, and it made me feel disenfranchised, like I was being used by them simply to get to Billie. When this became transparent to me, I found it irritating on several levels.

Finally the last straw came. I had a boyfriend from when I lived in Clovis, New Mexico, before we moved to England and came to Los

Angeles. He and I had amazing chemistry and he had always been in my heart. But I found that he was much more interested in hanging out with Billie than with me.

I don't think Billie was trying to hurt me by befriending and hanging out with them, but I definitely saw through it all and decided I needed to distance myself from the crazy mixed-up world of Hollywood. It was all getting to be too much of a soap opera for me. After a while this whole routine had grown a bit old, and I was "over" the Hollywood lifestyle, and I became restless for a change of pace.

Meanwhile my stepfather's extra two years of being stationed in England were over, and they moved back to the United States, settling in Montana. They had come back in 1976, so I decided to move back in with mom and Jack in 1977. After Hollywood, Montana was quite a contrast to say the least, but I was ready for something new.

CHAPTER THREE

A Family In Transition

MY mom and Jack had moved to Great Falls, Montana, from England. After feeling so confused and restless in California I made the decision to settle back into the small town world that I had been accustomed to living.

I moved back in with mom and Jack, and we all lived together on the military base, along with my two half-sisters Donna and Denise, who I had grown up with. I got a job at the base, working at the commissary. It wasn't long before I developed my own circle of friends there.

I had a comfortable life in Great Falls. When I was 21 I met Karl, the man who was to become my first husband. He was in the military at the time and was a rebound from a bad recent breakup. Karl's roommate Scott was dating my friend Shéree. When Karl and I got married in February of 1979, Sheree was my maid-of-honor. We had all lived together before Karl and I got married.

Dad flew up for the ceremony, and he gave me away. That was a really special time in my life as I had all my half-siblings in the wedding. I did not want to leave anyone out. There was Kelli, Travis and Kane – with whom I shared the same dad, and there was Donna and Denise – with whom I shared the same mom.

I do remember that dad gave me an ultimatum, claiming that Sarah would not come to my wedding if Billie was invited to attend. There was no way I would have even considered not inviting Billie, since she had been such a big part of my life and her three kids were in my wedding. So Sarah didn't come. However, that was totally by her choice, and not because I didn't invite her.

It was so funny as dad came up to Montana in a private plane, and Billie had him bring our wedding presents on his plane and a whole trash bag full of tin cans on strings to attach to our car bumper when the bride and groom made their exit. I thought that was absolutely hysterical.

At my wedding Billie sat next to dad on the front row, and my mom sat next to Billie. Well, dad sang at my wedding. He sang 'The Lord's Prayer'. He had been chewing gum, and when it was time to go and sing, he took the gum out of his mouth, opened Billie's hand, and put the gum in it.

My mom said the look on Billie's face was absolutely priceless! Remember, he and Billie were barely speaking to each other at this point in their lives.

Billie even sent my mom a 'thank you' note for having all of them at her house. That was so very sweet!

At this point, my relationship with my dad was on real sporadic terms. He was in his own little world and his new marriage with Sarah. With every one of dad's marriages and relationships, I had to continually find my own way into my father's life. He never has made it easy, and it was always me who had to take the initiative.

Dad is the kind of a man who has always gone straight from one relationship into the next one. There has never been a break for him in between affairs, relationships, or marriages. As soon as he divorced mom back in New Mexico, he was already involved with Billie. While he was with Billie, he had already started up with Sarah, and while married to Sarah, he began his affair with Tanya Tucker, and as soon as that began to cool off, Kim was already having a relationship with him. In that way, I have had to constantly redefine where I fit into all of this.

By now, I was married to Karl. Ours was a marriage that really went on longer than it should have. Ultimately, we were together for 16 years. Looking back on my life with Karl, I can honestly say that we never should have gotten married, but we did. We had three beautiful kids together, so I guess that it worked out the way that it should have.

I was six months pregnant when I got married, and I gave birth to my daughter Jenny in April of 1979. Right after my daughter was born my stepdad had gotten his orders to go to Germany, and my mother announced that she didn't want to go, because I had given birth to her first grandchild and she didn't want to leave the United States. So Karl put in for a transfer to a military base in Europe that was the closest to Germany.

We ended up in Aviano, Italy, for the next four years, which wasn't too bad of a drive from where mom and Jack were in Germany. Before we moved to Italy, and right after my daughter was born, I flew down to Los Angeles to see dad and Sarah. That was actually the last time I saw Sarah with him as a married couple.

So, not long after we got married, we moved to Italy. What happened is that the military stationed Karl there and in July of 1979 – six months after we were married – and all of a sudden I was living in Europe again.

Aviano was wonderful. I just fell in love with Italy: the food, the people, the scenery. Located 50 miles north of Venice, Aviano is situated near the southern part of the Italian Alps. Also, the Air Force base there was very family oriented. Dad did come to England for another tour while we were living in Europe, so we flew up from Italy to England to see him.

Meanwhile, back in America, a lot had happened in dad's life. He and Sarah had a son together, Dillon. Not long afterward their marriage broke up, and he had met Tanya Tucker.

Dad's whole – very public – 15-month affair with Tanya Tucker happened in the early eighties, and I had thankfully been in Italy for the majority of that drama. Apparently, it was Tanya who sought out dad. According to him, Tanya got wind of the fact that he was splitting up from Sarah, so she phoned him and said, "I want to help you. You could use a friend." Well, from what I understand, that was the start of it.

"T" was what everyone called Tanya at the time. In the press dad described "T" as being "an incurable party girl incapable of faithfulness". He also admitted, "I began dating and sleeping with Tanya before my divorce from Sarah was final."

Part of the press scandal they caused was due to the fact that when they started going out together dad was 44 years old, and Tanya had just turned 21. She had been making hit records since she was just 14 years old, so in her eyes she was already a middle-aged woman, and the minute she turned legal drinking age, she was ready to let loose.

I pretty much heard all about their relationship through my relatives, how wonderful it was, and how tumultuous it was as well. Apparently, when Tanya went back home with dad to meet his relatives, she fit well into the whole Arkansas crowd, because she loved to fish and do all of that simple kind of stuff, since that was how she grew up.

I remember talking to Tanya on the phone one time when Karl and I were living overseas. I had dad on the phone, and he put Tanya on the line and I talked to her, and my daughter talked to her as well. So, that whole relationship had come and gone when I wasn't even around.

Dad once said, "Dating Tanya to escape cocaine was like jumping into a lake to avoid getting wet."

They were also famous for their public arguments with each other, and when dad threatened to end his affair with Tanya, she made an unsuccessful suicide attempt. During one of their fights in New York City's Plaza Hotel, they managed to pull the drapes off of the wall, and the hotel fined dad $1,200 in damages. From what I understand, dad certainly had a wild time with Tanya. That was an understatement to say the least!

Meanwhile back in Italy, it didn't take long for me to find out that Karl and I weren't very attuned to each other. I decided that I wanted to leave him there and come back to the States, because I just couldn't take it anymore.

Unfortunately, I found myself in a very odd place. My mom and step-father at this point were stationed in Germany, and I didn't want to move in with them on another military base.

I didn't know where I was going to go. Naturally, I thought of dad first. I was never really sure what kinds of personal problems that my dad was going through at that time, because I had been thousands of miles away in Italy. When I came back to the States, I found that my dad was still strung out on drugs and alcohol.

This would have been in 1981. I remember calling dad's manager, Stan, to find out where dad was. Stan said to me, "Your dad doesn't want to talk to anyone."

I said to him, "Stan, I have to talk to my dad."

So, I got the phone number from him. When I called dad, he answered the telephone by yelling, "Who is this!?"

"It's Debby, dad, your daughter."

He said, "I don't care who this is, I said I don't want to be disturbed by anybody!" This was the height of his "substance abuse" phase, so I had to resign myself to the fact that he was a grown man, and he would have to find his way out of it himself.

Of course that was a very traumatic revelation for me. I was hoping to come to the States to stay with my dad, but clearly he was in no shape for that. So, I went to Arkansas instead because that was the only place I had to go, and I stayed at grandma and grandpa's for a little while. Then I went to stay with my aunt Barb who lived about an hour or an hour-and-a-half from my grandparents.

Finally I thought to myself, "Maybe I should go back to Italy and see if I can make this work with Karl?" So, I packed up my bags and I headed back to Italy, where I tried to make another go at my marriage.

I had only been back in the United States for a month or two, and this would have been in 1981. Not long after returning to Karl, I gave birth to my son Jesse, who was born in Italy in 1982.

At this point dad, on the rebound from Tanya Tucker, had already met the woman who was going to be his fourth wife, Kim Wollen. Ironically, Kim is exactly the same age as Tanya, which is two years younger than I am. They got married on October 25, 1982 and my half-brother Cal was born on April 19, 1983. We all knew she was pregnant at the time of their wedding.

Then Karl and I came back to the United States in 1983. He was now stationed in Colorado Springs, where my son Jeremy was born in 1984. Since my stepfather Jack had been in the military, and I had then married a man in the Air Force, much of my early life was dictated by the decisions of the military. We remained in Colorado until 1987.

By this point we had decided that our marriage was doomed, especially after the many arguments we had. The finishing touch came when he told me that the only reason he ever married me in the first place was because I was Glen Campbell's daughter. I am sure he said it in the midst of one of our many arguments, but nonetheless it hit me like a ton of bricks. Try as I might I couldn't really get our marriage back on track once I had heard something like that. I was never able to shake it from that moment on.

Karl was getting out of the military and had secured a job in California with Northrop. This was 1987 and dad had been living in Phoenix for many years now. He had bought a house and I believe Tanya had stayed there with him, and then when they broke up and he married Kim that is where they lived for a few more years. I felt that the most stabilizing thing I could do for my three children would be to move near my dad, their grandfather. That is why I moved to Phoenix. My mom and stepdad were still in Germany where they stayed for a few more years.

Karl was living in California, and our marriage was still suffering greatly but I wasn't ready to divorce him yet. After watching both of my parents divorce a couple of times I was determined to break this cycle. I can't say whether it was a good thing or a bad thing, but nonetheless it seemed worth fighting, for especially for my three kids. I was happy to move to Phoenix, where I began looking for work.

At this time, dad and I didn't have much of a relationship at all. I was his daughter, and he was my dad. I knew that I loved him, and that he loved me. But as far as having a rapport, or an actual relationship, it was pretty much non-existent.

Needless to say, when it came to defining my role in my dad's life, I felt "lost in the shuffle". My attempts at having a "father/daughter" relationship with dad – up to this point – were "hit or miss" at best. I was constantly trying to find a sense of belonging somewhere.

It was always great when I did see dad, but we really weren't that connected. And, when you are that young, you really aren't thinking about it. If you grew up in a normal home, and you were having issues with your parents, you might dwell on things that are going on at the time. But when you have all of this drama and interaction magnified by show business and other entertainers, and other children by other wives, and living much of your life on the road, it all gets a bit muddled together. I was just trying to find my way around any kind of relationship with my father that I could establish and have, like I had done my entire life.

I was now a married adult with three kids of my own, whose own relationship had crumbled. Dad and I were both in different spaces in our lives, and we didn't know that much about each other at this point.

It wasn't that my relationship with dad at this time was "odd", it was the only relationship that I had ever had with him: on-again and off-again. I had simply come to accept that as the norm. I was just trying to fit into dad's world, the same way that everyone else in his life was trying to find a way to fit into dad's world.

CHAPTER FOUR

Returning To Dad's Life

IT was 1987, and I found myself living in the Phoenix area, and my relationship with my father was officially a developing "work in progress". My three kids and I were living in an apartment in Chandler, which is just south of Scottsdale. I needed to support myself, so I started working as a school bus driver, which was something I had done before. I had driven a school bus for four years in Italy, and then I did it again for three years in Colorado, so it was something that was easy for me to do. I later landed another bus-driving job at another local school district, so I did that in Arizona for a while as well.

Being a school bus driver is the perfect job to have when you have kids. You work in the morning, and you work in the afternoon, and you are basically on the same schedule as your kids.

I finally arrived at the mindset of getting a divorce, because I was tired of making this relationship work, when it was clearly not working for either of us. Since Karl and I were planning on divorcing, and I needed to get health insurance for my kids, I had to have a job at all times.

Not long afterward, I applied for a job at one of the major airlines, and I was hired as a customer service representative. You could work at the gates – boarding the airplane; at the ticket counter – selling tickets and checking bags; on the phone – taking reservations; on the ramp – loading the airplane and marshalling it to the gate when it landed; provisioning the aircraft – with all the service items; or flying the friendly skies – as a flight attendant. One day I could be at a ticket counter, and the next day in the air. It really was a diversified job to say the least. Eventually they decided to make it one or the other: a flight attendant, or on the ground. You made more money flying as there was extra overnight pay, so in the air I went, and this began my lifelong career as an airline employee.

Karl and I continued to give our marriage a "go" again, and dad helped us with a down payment on a house in Tempe, Arizona. This began our vacillating phase of: "Are we getting a divorce?"/"Should we give it another try?" Unfortunately it was a phase that dragged on for many years. Although we both knew it was over, we never officially got divorced until 1996.

In September of 1987, dad was performing a concert here at the Coliseum in Phoenix. It was part of the Arizona State Fair, and I said to him, "Dad, I want to sing with you."

And he said, "OK."

That was how it all started. I was 31 years old at the time. The next thing I knew, there I was onstage with him at the Arizona State Fair. And so began our *real* journey as a father and daughter. The first song that we performed onstage together was 'Burning Bridges', which was his very first Top 20 Country hit, back in 1966. I sang with him, and then I would harmonize on the chorus. It worked out beautifully.

I will never forget that performance. I was so nervous that I literally shook onstage, and I am certain that you could hear it in my voice. I remember that my kids were out in the audience watching their mother and their grandfather up onstage together. My nervousness was never due to the fact that dad was a huge singing star. I never looked at dad like that. To me, he was just my dad. Of course I was a bit intimidated, because dad is such a perfectionist. While he is a huge perfectionist, in the same breath if he didn't think that I had the talent to do it he would have never allowed me onstage to do it.

It was quite exhilarating to say the least, and after we got off stage, he had nothing but praise for me.

It was such an awesome experience, and of course I loved doing it. I knew that I could sing, but I had never really done it professionally. When I was younger I had sung with a group called Sky People. It has never been "my calling in life" or anything, I just knew that I could get up in front of people and sing. Whenever I had the opportunity to sing in front of other people, they would always give me positive feedback and say things like: "Oh, you really have a great voice. You should be a professional singer."

Up until that point, all I had wanted to be was a "mom" and bake cookies for my kids when they came home from school. I always wanted to have the perfect family like the ones depicted on the all-American sixties TV programs *Leave It To Beaver* and *The Donna Reed Show*. Who knows if that was really perfect in reality or not, but it sure looked like perfection to me! That was all that I wanted to do, up until this time.

However, after that one September night and singing that one song 'Burning Bridges' live onstage with dad, I was hooked. I knew right then and there that I wanted to sing more. Although I was still basically an "at home mom", I had officially been bitten by "the performing bug". I was thrilled to find that dad was more than welcome to the idea.

After that night, dad said to me, "Honey, you can come out on the road and sing with me anytime you want." Of course, I had another job at that point – working for the airlines – so I wasn't able to do it all the time. But with his encouragement, I would go out on the road with dad every once in a while, and slowly I started to become a regular part of his show.

It was an arrangement that worked out so naturally. It was enjoyable for both of us. First of all, it was an opportunity for me to get closer to my father after all of these years, and he liked it too. I soon found that – even more important than it just being fun – was that fact that it became an inroad towards finally having a real relationship with dad.

We had finally found something in common that we both could do together. We had such an on-again/off-again father-and-daughter relationship for all of those years, I felt that I could finally feel like I was actually a genuine part of my father's life and not just "the child from a former marriage". Singing together was something that we could share.

It worked out perfectly from the very start. He could have a family member out on the road with him, and I could finally have a relationship with my father again. That very first year in California, at maybe the second or third concert that I performed at with dad, all of the nervousness disappeared and I found myself getting up on stage with true confidence and ease. I remember that we were in Whittier, California.

The way it all evolved was that I just happened to be on an overnight stay with the airline in Orange County, California, and dad was performing there. When I got off of the plane there was a limousine waiting there to pick me up, and take me over to the show. It was an outdoor festival, and Eddie Rabbitt was on the bill that night as well. It was a big country music festival, because it was the weekend of the Fourth of July, and there were a lot of people on the bill.

I met MaryAnne Beaman and her husband Mike at this concert. They were friends with Bill – dad's tour manager – and his wife Holly. MaryAnne heard me singing with dad and she said to me, "You've got a great voice! Let me see if I can get you some bookings on your own as a vocalist." I found that very encouraging, and it further cemented my desire to keep singing professionally with my father.

That night I sang two or three songs. According to MaryAnne, "I remember Glen being really proud to have his daughter up onstage with him. And, he also boasted a lot about the merits of the airline. He said up onstage, 'Oh my daughter works for the airlines!' He was so proud of that and he just beamed when he introduced Debby onstage that night."

At this point, I was the only one of his kids who actually showed an aptitude and an interest in singing, so I think that made him proud too. Within dad's show, I started out singing the one song 'Burning Bridges' with him, but it wasn't long before we started singing 'Let It Be Me' as well. 'Let It Be Me' had been a Top 40 duet hit for dad and Bobbie Gentry, so it became a natural choice for me to do it with him. I also sang a couple of solo songs as well. I did Patsy Cline's 'Crazy' and a Loretta Lynn song too. Along the way we also performed a duet version of 'United We Stand'.

After that, I started traveling with dad more frequently. In 1988 I performed with him at the Roy Clark Theater in Branson, Missouri. Those particular bookings were four-or-five day gigs, and that year we were booked there six times.

Little did I know at the time, but Branson was to be the scene of some of the best and some of the most rewarding times of my life, and the height of my relationship with my father.

CHAPTER FIVE

Mansion In Branson

IN the early nineties dad signed an agreement to perform several times in Branson at the Grand Palace Theater, to alternate hosting duties with Louise Mandrell. So, whenever dad sang at the Grand Palace, he was always part of a "double bill". Either it was dad and another headliner, or it was Louise Mandrell and another headliner. While onstage they would be playing host to the other acts. It would be Glen and Waylon Jennings, or Glen and the Oaks Ridge Boys, Glen and the Statler Brothers, or Glen and Marie Osmond.

One year Marie was sick, or cancelled for a personal reason, and that's when dad had me step in as the opening act for his show that particular year. I instantly agreed to do it, but even though I had been singing now for a couple of years I still was very nervous at first. I was only given a couple of days to prepare, and with the help of dad's band, and his musical director TJ Kuenster, we were able to get it done. TJ is absolutely incredible. I call him the "Mighty Maestro". He is such a brilliant talent.

TJ and I went through a potential list of songs, we looked at the charts and decided on the musical keys that were the best for me, and we put together a whole 30 to 40 minute set list. My set consisted of cover tunes of various artists such as Patsy Cline, Trisha Yearwood, Patty Loveless, Wynonna Judd and so on. I would have loved to have done a Tanya Tucker song or two as I love her voice and she had some great songs, but that wasn't happening while I was in dad's show. And then I still did the same amount of songs and duets in dad's portion of the show.

Sometimes my aunts and uncles would also come up to Branson from Arkansas and dad would of course want them singing on the stage with him. It truly was a family affair which dad absolutely loved.

My cousin Steve, whose dad is my dad's brother, would also sing every time he came to Branson. I really think that is when dad was most happy: when he had all his family together in his show. I know my grandmother and grandfather would have been smiling down from heaven to see how he included so many members of the family in his show over the years.

For anyone who hasn't been to Branson, it is a town that sits in the majestic Ozark Mountains, surrounded by some beautiful lakes: Table Rock, Taneycomo, and Bull Shoals. My family and I enjoyed many great times on Table Rock Lake on pontoon boats, which everyone referred to as "party barges". They have lots of theaters in Branson with a variety of different family oriented shows, as well as big production shows. It is very similar to Las Vegas, although there is absolutely no gambling. That is not to say that some folks haven't tried to bring gambling into the area, but since Branson is considered to be located in the middle of the "Bible Belt" of America, that will probably never happen. For that reason it is considered to be the capital of "family entertainment" in the Midwest, and Branson attracts millions of visitors every year. It was an ideal place for dad to base his show for several years.

When Waylon Jennings played with dad at the Grand Palace, he fell absolutely in love with my eight-year-old son Jeremy and he even had a jacket especially made for him like the one Waylon had with the big "W" on the back, and he had Jeremy's name put on the front of it. I thought that was so nice of him to do. And, I will never forget the impressive Indian statue that Waylon had onstage too.

Another act that I loved who played at the Grand Palace was the Oak Ridge Boys. They always brought a ping pong table with them on the road, so my kids loved playing with everyone: the crew, the Oaks, and with each other. It truly was a magical time for all of us during those years. And of course the food was catered in between shows, so we all ate as a family too.

A lot of other top country acts were booked there too, and I have great memories of them from those days, including Lee Greenwood, Mark Chesnutt, Don Williams, and Eddie Rabbitt. I even remember going bungee cord jumping with some of Lee Greenwood's band members. We all had so much fun.

I was also the opening act for dad when he headlined at the Golden Nugget in Las Vegas. He was more comfortable having me opening the show than he was with anyone else. Whenever a concert promoter wanted to put him on the bill, he would regularly just say, "Well, then just let Debby sing a few songs before my set." And, that was because he preferred it that way.

If dad was, say, doing a show in Tucson and they wanted an opening act he was unfamiliar with, he just hated it. That was because the opening band would tune the equipment the way they wanted it, and it would mess it all up for dad and his band. So, a lot of times, that's where I came into the show. I could perform as the opening act with dad's band, and then we would introduce dad for his part of the show, and the equipment wouldn't have to be changed or altered.

Before I came into the show, dad's regular opening act had been his backing band, the Jeff Dayton Band. Then when I started singing with dad, someone had told me that Jeff complained I was taking his place. They said they told him, "When your daughter gets old enough and wants to sing with you, then you'll understand."

I never intended on stepping on anyone's toes, when I suddenly became a recurring and regular opening act. I didn't want to take the spotlight away from Jeff or anyone for that matter. I was more intent on being an active part of my dad's life.

At this point, I had my own list of songs that I would do as a solo performer, and there were also the duet songs that I could come onstage and sing with dad.

During the Branson era, sadly I lost some of the most beloved people in my life. One of the most surprising ones was my own grandmother, who died December 31, 1991.

I remember my best friend MaryAnne calling me and asking me if I was flying to Arkansas. I said to her, "Why would I fly to Arkansas?"

And she said, "Because your grandma died."

"What?" I replied in shock. "My grandma died? You're kidding? Are you sure?"

"Yeah, I am sure," she said.

I called dad, and I said, "Dad, did Grandma die?"

He said, "Yeah, two days ago."

"You're kidding me? Two days ago? Are you *kidding* me? And I am just hearing about it from somebody else, other than family? My friend MaryAnne had to be the one who told me that my own grandmother had died?"

Dad never called me to tell me. He was too busy golfing in Phoenix to have picked up the phone! I was amazed.

I was so upset and so mad at my dad. They had a private plane that was going to take them to Arkansas. However my Aunt Sandy and Uncle Ed were here in Phoenix at the time, so there wasn't enough room for me to go back with them on the private plane. I was pretty upset with that. This was my dad's mother, and I wasn't at all happy to miss her funeral.

In 1993, when I found out that Billie had terminal cancer, it was a total shock. I distinctly remember when Billie was dying, it was truly one of the saddest things that I have ever gone through. I went and sat at her bedside for two weeks. I remember Kim calling me from Phoenix and saying to me, "You'd better get back here to Arizona! You don't have any business over there."

I said to her, "Oh yes I do have business here. This woman was a major part of my life, and she's dying, and I'm here to make my peace with her, and help out with Kelli and the kids if they need me to do anything. I am here to help them get through their mom dying of cancer!"

Billie had breast cancer, and it just spread throughout her entire body. It was weird, because Billie had little cancer spots removed from her, and we'd always wondered if it had anything to do with the house that they lived in. It was located right underneath a radio tower. But I also know that Billie's grandmother had breast cancer, and it seemed to be exactly the same.

Poor Billie. She had a morphine patch inserted in her to release a dose of the medication whenever she needed it. I remember sitting there at her bedside. I will never forget it.

She was talking to people who were standing behind me. However, there was no one standing behind me. But she was so high on morphine that she was convinced she saw them.

While I was there with her I told her everything that came to my mind. I didn't want her to leave this Earth and then to have later regretted not telling her everything that I wanted her to know. I told her how I felt about her, and that I loved her very much. I was able to thank her for allowing me to be such an important part of not only dad's life but hers too.

I explained to her how devastating it was for dad to have told me not to speak to Billie anymore. "I never wanted to *not* be friends with you after you and dad divorced," I said, "but I was told that this was what I had to do."

I also told her that I thought that she didn't want me in her life, because I wasn't her real daughter. Not once did I feel that since she and dad had divorced she didn't have to be around me anymore.

She told me that she felt the exact same reciprocal thing. She said that she thought that I didn't want her in my life anymore.

Billie told actress Lindsay Wagner's mom, Marilyn Ball, "I wish I would have known how Debby felt all these years, I would have a done a lot more for her."

I sat with her throughout this horrifyingly tragic ordeal, yet her own daughter did not. My sister Kelli and Billie had a very estranged relationship, as most mothers and daughters do at some point. Kelli was never able to make her peace with her mom, which I thought was so tragic.

I had said to her, "Kelli, you have to sit with your mom."

Finally she came around to seeing my point, but it was unfortunately too late. Kelli was literally going to do that the very next day, but her mom died that night.

I was in shock when she died. I remember Billie had been cancer-free in November, and she died of it the next February. Apparently, when it came back, it came back very aggressively. She ended up dying at Marilyn's house in Malibu. Marilyn's daughter Lindsay was actually the babysitter for all of Billie's kids. After she died I was able to return to my life in Phoenix with a clear conscience that I had said everything that I needed to say to her.

Singing with dad in Branson gave me the opportunity to meet some truly great people. Loretta Lynn was one of them. She is so sweet, and talented. Loretta is someone who is truly without pretense. If she likes you, she speaks up and says so. And if she doesn't like something that you are doing, she speaks her mind too.

I remember the first time I met Loretta. She said to me, "I never liked Glen Campbell, because when I found out that he had another child from another marriage, and he never mentioned her [meaning me] and I just never liked him for that."

It made me feel good on one hand for Loretta to feel that way, however it made me feel bad that she didn't like dad. How could anyone not like my dad? He is so nice and humble. Yet, it felt good to have Loretta stick up for me, even without my knowing her.

A lot of people don't realize that dad has something to do with the success of country music superstar Alan Jackson. Dad ran into Alan's wife, Denise, in an airport one day. She was a flight attendant, and she told dad that her husband was a country songwriter, so he gave her a business card for Marty Gamblin at the Nashville office.

Dad had a music publishing company in Nashville, and Marty Gamblin ran it. Alan gave Marty a phone call, and Alan and Marty became good friends. After that Marty helped Alan secure a position in dad's publishing company. Alan wrote several songs, and he ended up recording them. Then he ended up becoming a famous million-selling recording artist, and dad made royalties off of all of that publishing.

That was the connection with Alan Jackson. Eventually, Alan bought all of his songs back, for a "pretty penny" I am sure, but I have no idea exactly how much money exchanged hands. Dad also owned some of the songs written by Brian White, and there was also a band that dad had signed to his management company, but their career didn't turn out to be at all successful, especially when compared to the huge country superstar that Alan Jackson became.

I wasn't involved in dad's publishing or management companies, but I certainly knew that he owned parts of all sorts of entertainment oriented companies. I never got involved in any of that.

I remember Tanya Tucker doing a show at the Grand Palace. Dad wanted to go see her, so we did. We were sitting in the audience and during her show she had a "wardrobe malfunction". It was quite comical, as dad said to us who were sitting with him, "Does anyone have a safety pin?"

We came up with one, and dad got up out of his seat and walked up to the front of the stage and handed her the safety pin. It was quite a sight to see for us, as well as the audience, *and* Tanya herself!

I remember on one occasion I was in Pebble Beach, California, with dad. He was playing in the Skins Game golf tournament with Clint Eastwood. He went into his golf bag and pulled something out of one of the pockets and came over and said, "I've got something for you." It was his ring that my grandmother used to wear. It was a gold ring with his name – Glen – spelled out in diamonds. He got it back when my grandmother died. Since then I have had it forever, and it is one of my most prized possessions.

When we were all living in Branson, there were of course some behind-the-scenes family dramas as well. Dad would have a whole Beach

Boys segment in his show. This was because he had played guitar on so many of the Beach Boys' greatest hits. In the middle of the show, they would do a whole big skit highlighting the music of the Beach Boys. There would be an elaborate set with waves breaking, and there was a little shark fin that swam across the backdrop. It was a really clever and well-staged segment of the show.

There was also a lifeguard chair as part of the Beach Boys stage set, with the four boys – Cal, Jesse, Shannon, and Jeremy, and I think Ashley as well – all taking turns in the chair playing the lifeguard. They were just little kids back then, and they got a big kick out of it.

However, the Beach Boys skit presented a situation that caused one of my first fights with my dad. It was my son Jeremy's turn to do the lifeguard role. Jeremy was about six or seven years old at the time.

Dad came over to me and said, "Jeremy can't do it. He doesn't clap in the right parts."

I said, "Dad, are you kidding? Did you just say that 'he doesn't clap in the right parts,' in the middle of a song where the music is so loud and there is so much going on?"

I remember my brother, Shannon, saying, "But dad, it's Jeremy's turn."

However, dad had made his decision, and there was absolutely no arguing with him at times like these.

I got so mad at this point, and I said, "You are actually going to tell your seven-year-old grandson that he can't sit in the lifeguard chair because he doesn't clap in the right parts!?!"

I was simply not OK with that. In fact I was so upset that I left the theater. I didn't do the show that night either. I was out in the parking lot, sitting in my car crying. I could not believe that my father would tell my seven-year-old he can't be in the show! Furthermore, it wasn't as if anyone was paying any attention to the seven-year-old on the lifeguard chair. But that was just what a perfectionist my father is and was onstage.

After that showdown, I was convinced that I was all finished with the show at that point. I could tell that I was going to be fired the next day. So, the next day came, and no one called me and told me that I was fired. The next night I went to the theater, and it was like nothing had happened.

This was just another example of dad putting family members in his show. When my aunts and uncles would come to Branson, he would always put them in the show. My brother Cal would play drums. In the

Christmas show, it was my little brother Cal who would play drums during the song 'Little Drummer Boy'.

Since Arkansas is only a four-hour drive away, there were always Campbell family members coming to Branson. Dad loved having them up onstage with him. At the time the Grand Palace was *the* place to play in Branson. It was the biggest and the most prestigious place in town. It had 4,500 seats, and it was wired for television production as well. In fact, lots of TV specials were taped there. If you were headlining the Grand Palace in Branson, then you were a big deal in town that is for sure!

I had such a great time in Branson, and at one point, I even had my own show as a headliner there. It was called *The Branson Morning Round-Up*. It was a live theater show, but it was in the morning. People would come to town on tours, and we would have musical guests. Actually, there were two morning shows in town at that time. One of them was Bob Nichols' show, the other mine. It was a variety show setup, and I would sing in it. The show went on for four or five months. We were ahead of our time on the morning circuit. My friend MaryAnne worked on it. This was an era – in the early nineties – when several other entertainers started showing up in Branson as well.

Since Branson is a very family-oriented town, which each year attracts millions of visitors, it was the ideal place for dad to have based his show for several years. For dad and I, this was just the beginning of big things happening there.

CHAPTER SIX

The Glen Campbell Goodtime Theater And Beyond

AFTER playing the Grand Palace so successfully for over three years, dad received an invitation to open his own theater. What happened was that developers came into town and built a theater, and then they paid him to put his name on it, so that it became the Glen Campbell Goodtime Theater. It was owned by a Branson investment group; Lee Iacocca of Chrysler Motor Company was also a part of that group. It really was an awesome entertainment venue. At that point, I really became a staple in the middle of *The Glen Campbell Show*.

The era in which dad had the Glen Campbell Goodtime Theater was from 1993 to 1996. I have so many great memories of those years, and we were able to stage some really significant events. We held *The Jerry Lewis Telethon* there in 1995 and 1996, which I orchestrated with dad – the whole telecast and everything. I was responsible for booking the talent, and for making the arrangements to get all of the food set up backstage.

The telethon had dozens of guest-starring acts on it. We had Tony Orlando, Jim Stafford, and all of the acts that were in town at that time. It was a lot of fun to do. Fortunately, we didn't have to fly people in to perform on it. Instead we utilized everyone who was headlining in Branson that particular Labor Day weekend.

Debra Moreno-Lowther and I also arranged a fundraiser for the victims of the Oklahoma City bombing in 1995. That was really gratifying too, knowing that we were doing some good for others. In fact, we did a lot of events there that were staged for charitable causes.

I organized a bowling tournament one time and the Glen Campbell

Goodtime Theater played against all the other venues and we had quite a few participants. The team players included crew members, sound engineers, the artists, and pretty much anyone who wanted to participate could. Dad even bowled, as well as Charley Pride and his wife Rozene. We even had prizes donated for the winners. That was such a totally normal thing for dad to participate in and there were many more fun experiences for us ahead.

One year we tried to come up with a morning show that we could incorporate bingo into, as MaryAnne and I both loved to play bingo. But we just couldn't quite figure out how to make the concept work as there is no gambling in Branson (although I don't consider bingo gambling).

In the days of the Glen Campbell Goodtime Theater, it was a very family-oriented routine. At one point I moved my entire family there. We were singing in the theater for three weeks at a time and then I still had to fulfill my 40 hours a month obligation to the airlines. If I didn't move there, I would never see my kids, so we packed up and moved to Branson.

I was still married to Karl. Or, as I describe it: I was still part of this tumultuous marriage. It seemed like our marriage continued to be "on" and "off" and then back "on" again. This was how our entire marriage was for the duration of it. Karl moved to Branson too, but I felt that it was his decision as to whether or not he did that. At this point I couldn't have cared less if he was part of the picture or not. When I moved there I told him, "You can move too if you want to, and if you don't want to, that's fine too."

It was a great arrangement at the Glen Campbell Goodtime Theater, as we did two shows some days. They would cater food for us in between events, so we didn't have to leave between the shows. The school bus would drop my kids off at the theater after school, and we would have dinner together, and they would hang out for a while and go home. I would do the evening show and then I would go home. So, that would be our routine for weeks at a time.

The concert was constructed like a TV variety show. Dad would open with a big musical number, and then he would introduce his guest stars, and then he would leave the stage. Then he would do some more solo numbers, and then he would introduce me again, and I would come back onstage and sing duets with him.

Dad grew to hate this show, and he complained that it was like doing a

TV show. We had dancers, and all of these elaborate sets that we would use. He would have much preferred making it a family affair, in which he would have had his sisters and brothers – my aunts and uncles – in the show. It was dad's wife Kim, along with his manager Stan, who was really turning this into a whole production number. This was not something that my dad wanted, but he went along with it, because that is what Kim and Stan wanted him to do.

As more and more performers came into Branson, shows had to compete with each other, and the production values and the volume of production numbers increased consistently. In the later incarnations of dad's show there were some grand production numbers that were totally over-the-top. Using his religious songs like 'No More Night', and featuring Apocalypse-like Christian productions that ended with angels flying in the sky, he definitely created a certain "wow" factor.

Dad used to do a lot of gospel numbers in his show, and regularly began featuring more and more religious music. In fact many of his albums during this era were based on Christian music. His album *No More Night* had won him a gospel music Dove Award in 1986, and his gospel song 'Where Shadows Never Fall' won him another Dove Award in 1992. He later won his third Dove Award for his year 2000 Album of the Year winner: *A Glen Campbell Christmas*. So, dad's music was very often rooted in the Christian music market.

In the early stages of getting things running at the Glen Campbell Goodtime Theater, there was an incident with the rules of the concession stand. I remember sitting down with the manager of concessions. They had said that Glen and his family and his children wouldn't have to pay for anything to eat or drink, but everyone else would. That was all good until I went to purchase something and I was told I had to pay. It wasn't the paying for something that I was upset about. It was the fact that I was specifically told "Glen and his kids do not have to pay for anything". Since I am his kid (no matter what my age was) I wanted the manager to tell me how I didn't fit into this scenario. She couldn't of course. I was so mad and put off by it, that the concessions lady just decided to make dad and everyone pay. But mind you: it was like a quarter here or there. However, in my mind it was the principle!

Although there was sometimes built-up stress, it really was a great period in our lives. And the most important aspect of all of this was that I had dad actively back in our lives. The issue of the battle for the "free popcorn" was meaningless compared to that bigger and more important fact.

The shows at the Glen Campbell Goodtime Theater were really elaborate productions that were fun to be a part of: there were singers and dancers, and Jim Barber the comedian was involved as well, so it was a really big extravaganza. Whenever my aunts – Aunt Sandy and Aunt Barb – were in town, they became part of the show too, as dad so sincerely loved performing with them.

At this point I wasn't just holding down two jobs – as a flight attendant, and part of dad's show – but I was also working in the office at the theater during the day as well. I was helping book tour buses and sending out mass mailings to the tour bus companies as well as raising a family. It was one of the busiest times in my life, but I absolutely loved it.

For the time being my marriage to Karl had – for both of us – become a mere "marriage of convenience". He ended up taking a job in Springfield, Missouri, about 45 minutes from Branson. (After our inevitable divorce, he stayed there.)

Meanwhile, in September of 1996 my granddaughter Morgan was born to my teenage daughter, Jenny. Morgan was only 5 pounds 11 ounces when she was born. She was very tiny, and my daughter had been toxemic.

At this time dad and I went on a short tour to England with Kenny Rogers and Tammy Wynette. When I returned from England my granddaughter was in the Branson Hospital. She had contracted whooping cough and was in a serious condition. She was dying, so we had her transferred to a hospital in Springfield and she came down with pneumonia and both of her lungs collapsed.

Morgan was in intensive care for two weeks. Jenny was 17 years old when she gave birth and she really had a hard time with motherhood: serious post-partum depression. She signed "power of attorney" over to me for custody of the baby, and I sat at the hospital every day with this tiny baby who had tubes coming out of her little helpless body. After she recovered, she required breathing treatments every four hours and round the clock oxygen. I asked my ex-husband if he could watch her on the weekends while I did my airline job but he said he couldn't commit, so I rented out my house in Branson and moved to Arizona to live with dad.

At that time, my son Jesse moved to Springfield with his dad, and my other son Jeremy came to Arizona with me.

Jenny stayed in Missouri with her friends, in hopes of finishing high school. And so, for the next year, I flew for the airlines while Morgan's other grandma cared for her. When dad and I sang on the road, we took Morgan with us. There were many nights when Morgan would sit on the side of the stage in her car seat listening to a great concert. Sometimes Jeremy would come with me to help take care of her. After about nine months of living in Arizona at dad's house, and getting Morgan on the road to recovery, we moved back to Branson to the house I still owned there. Dad and I had a tour to Australia coming up and I knew I couldn't skip the tour to take care of Morgan myself so I told my daughter, "Now is our time to see if you can be a mother."

My friends Marty and Tim stayed with my boys Jesse and Jeremy, and Jenny took Morgan. Before I left for Australia, I told my daughter, "I want you to take Morgan and try to be a mom to her. And when I get home from this trip, if you just feel that you are not 'mom material', then I will legally adopt her as my own. But if I adopt her, this will be something between you and me as mother and daughter, for the rest of our lives, and you won't be able to disappear, and then one day decide that you want her back."

Thankfully it all ended well for us. And, while I was away, Jenny became the mother that I hoped she would be. She has had Morgan ever since. It was a very stressful time in my life, but very rewarding.

That was just one of many things I have had to contend with, and it just grew from there. So eventually it led me to a couple of sessions with therapist Gary Smalley, to clear my head. It was probably inevitable that I would go into therapy sessions, with all I had been through up to this point. Actually, he validated my feelings and said this was not normal behavior for a family, and that I had every right to feel the way I was feeling.

This particular tour of Australia was also a great beginning of dad and me really having a one-on-one kind of "father and daughter" relationship. I have a beautiful opal ring that my dad bought for me when we were in Australia. On that trip we went to the Gold Coast of Australia, and dad and I did a lot of fun things together.

Dad spent so much time in Branson that he and Kim eventually built a house there. Then when he was done with the Glen Campbell Goodtime Theatre, his show took up residence at the Andy Williams "Moon River" Theatre. Around this time dad and Kim sold the Branson house, and now lived full time in Phoenix. When we moved to the Andy Williams "Moon River" Theatre, it once again reverted to being *The Glen Campbell Show*, with me as part of it.

Dad and I actually enjoyed quite a few shows together in those days. Some of the other headliners were George Jones, Lori Morgan, and Ronnie Milsap. We got to see a lot of wonderful acts, and every time we went to someone's show, dad would get up and perform with the artist. It was an extra treat for the audience as well as the artist too.

This was a time in my life when dad and I became closer than ever. On top of doing the shows in Branson, I also went out on tour with him. He didn't do a lot of touring when he had the theater. He was too busy doing that. And for him, he was able to have his days off to play golf all day if he wanted. Even on show days, he would play golf during the day and then go to the theater every night, just like he was commuting to a job that was close to home. He wouldn't have to pack up and travel to the next town after every show. The theater afforded him the opportunity not to have to be on the road all of the time, and still make money doing shows, and have his family close by, while still being able to play golf.

When we were in Branson, we had a great routine: get up, have breakfast, go golfing, go back to the condo and take a nap, get up, go have dinner, do a show. That was quite the schedule!

And if it was raining and golfing was "out", then I would have to find things for dad and me to do. "Hey, Arnold Palmer is opening a golf course up there, let's go up and see him," anything to do with golf, and dad was up for it. I came up with all sorts of projects and outings to keep dad occupied and entertained.

While performing at the Andy Williams "Moon River" Theatre after the shows we would spend a lot of time in Andy's private dressing room visiting with whichever group of friends was gathered there that evening. Andy's wife Debbie Williams, and his brother Don and Don's wife Jeanne were almost always there. Sometimes Dick and Dee Dee Gass, who was one of the Lennon Sisters, would be there too.

Since so many of these performers lived in Branson, we would go to Andy's house a lot, and we would go over to Don (Andy's brother) and

Jeanne Williams' home too. Don Williams – who is not to be confused with Don Williams the country singer – is a great cook. And, let me tell you: he thoroughly enjoyed entertaining. We would also spend a lot of fun times at Dick and Dee Dee's house.

Backstage in Andy's dressing room, I had the pleasure of meeting Ann-Margret, Shirley Jones, Ray Stevens, Bobby Vinton, Kitty Wells, Charo, Petula Clark, and many more wonderful entertainers. And, all of this time we spent together it was almost always just dad and I. Kim was not around much in those days.

Quite a few comments were made about that from other wives. Kim would only come in every once in a while, because – to be quite honest – she really didn't like Branson at all. On the other hand, dad loved it. He definitely enjoyed the simpler life. He actually would not have minded living there on a full-time basis. Since he was such an avid golfer, he could play golf every single day and sing at night and truly relax.

Without a doubt, the two most important women in dad's life at the time were me and his then wife Kim. Dad once said to me, "If any of my wives had been like you, I would have only been married once." I wasn't quite sure what that meant, but I certainly took it as a compliment. While Kim kept busy with raising her three children, or remodeling any one of their series of houses, I was often the one who spent the most time with him.

I was truly getting to spend a lot of one-on-one quality time together with dad. He and I were building a definite close and different kind of relationship than he had with any of my half-siblings. It was just a hanging out and having fun kind of relationship.

Kim was interviewed for a 1999 book called *Nashville Wives: Country Music's Celebrity Wives Reveal The Truth About Their Husbands And Marriages* by Mrs. George Jones and Tom Carter. My brother Travis suggested I read it, since he was living with dad at that time and I wasn't. In it Kim openly proclaimed that she prayed to God, and said out loud in her prayer: "Lord deliver me from this. Send me a Christian millionaire that I can be in love with and he can be in love with me!" She then went on to say, "I had one Jewish girlfriend and one Catholic girlfriend with me. They both looked at me and said, 'I can't believe you prayed like that'." Two weeks later she met dad. Then Kim was pregnant, and they got married.

My relationship with Kim during this era was never especially close. We hung out together a little bit at the beginning of her relationship with dad. Kim is two years younger than me, so it is a different kind of bond to begin with. I never really gave it that much thought. We would occasionally make jokes and cracks about our similar ages. We both had young kids at the same time, and we were all going to church together, so we actually had a lot in common. I didn't really hang out with her much when we all lived in Branson.

At the time, Kim and dad had a big house there, and my family and I were there too. Although my boys were basically the same age as Kim and dad's three kids, I was always aware of a separation between our two families. Clearly dad was the only "common denominator" in this picture.

I came to realize that dad and I are so very much alike. We are both very simple in our needs. It doesn't take a lot to please us. In my eyes too, I could see that underneath all of the show-business gloss, dad was just a very simple guy. He never liked waste or excess. He didn't have to have a lot of possessions to make him happy. When we were traveling, he wasn't impressed with huge hotel suites. He preferred a more compact room. He often wanted to go back to Arkansas to see his family members.

Dad was quite easy to please. I would say to him, "Hey, I'm going to go back to Arkansas with the kids. Why don't you go?" And he would enthusiastically agree. So often we would all go there – the 10 of us: me and my kids and he and Kim and his kids.

Although dad could sometimes get Kim to come to Arkansas, Kim would stay at Uncle Shorty's house. We would always hang out at Uncle Gerald's house and at the little creek that was on his land. Kim did go to the creek, but when we went up to the house dad would come up to Uncle Gerald's without her. We had a great time there. We would have a "jam session" with all of the family taking turns singing with the band my cousin Steve had with his sons.

Kim is originally from North Carolina, and from what she has said, she danced onstage with the Rockettes at Radio City Music Hall in New York City. Let's face it: there is a big difference between Manhattan and Arkansas! Maybe that is why she never seemed very keen on Arkansas.

Dad grew to be very comfortable with me and with my circle of friends. In fact, on occasion he would even hang out with me and my pals, that's how close we became. When dad and I were together, he could just be an "everyday Joe". He enjoyed the people I surrounded myself with.

Dad's fans are amongst the most die-hard fans on the planet. I recently ordered the DVDs of the TV series *The Midnight Special*, just to see dad on it. And as I sat watching it, there were his friends Lynnie and her mom Barb right in the front row. They have probably been around dad more than I have!

When it was just dad and me, I would make certain that some of his fans had access to him. Fans over the years would e-mail me at the Forum, which is a web-based site that fans could go to discuss all things Glen.

They would write things like, "I am going to be at such-and-such a show, and if it is at all possible, we would like to meet your dad after the show. We will be sitting in seats number so-and-so."

If they were people I knew, or recognized, I would go out before the show and find them and bring them backstage. Or I would let them know, "This is where you need to meet me after the show, and I will bring you back."

Dad was always good about doing those "meet & greet" events after the shows. He loved his fans, and he knew that he wouldn't be anything without them.

At one point, during dad's ongoing run at the Andy Williams "Moon River" Theatre, I decided to pack up and move to Las Vegas. I was ready for something new.

During this era, while I had such a great relationship with my dad, my relationship with my mother was a bit of a roller coaster. There was one point when my mom wasn't speaking to me for two years. She got this idea in her head that I loved my dad more than I loved her, because I was spending so much time with him, trying to have a relationship with him. She just – quite frankly – couldn't understand it, so she stopped talking to me for two years.

It was like I not only had to work to fit into my dad's life, but now I had to work to fit into my mom's life too. I remember when I moved back to Phoenix from Las Vegas, I moved in with my sister Denise. And my mom said to me, "I don't like you and Denise living together, because sometimes I just want to come over and visit them, and not have to visit all of you at the same time."

I thought to myself, "I could never say anything like this to one of my kids." And I remember feeling very hurt by that statement, but as always, I kept those feelings to myself.

This was just another example of me feeling that I was not fitting in anywhere. And here mom was talking about her two daughters! Finally, after two years, she ended up calling me in Branson. I remember answering the phone and saying, "Hello."

She said, "Hello. It's mom. I'm calling to say I'm sorry." Finally she wanted to make amends.

One year Sally Jesse Raphael brought her TV talk show to Phoenix and dad was her guest. Of course he recounted his marriages and said some uncomplimentary things about each of his past wives, my mom included. After she saw the program, mom was so upset with me about the things he said on camera.

I told her, "Mom do you really think I have any control on anything dad blurts out on national TV?"

One year dad and I sang the national anthem at a Phoenix Suns basketball game. I let my son Jeremy pick the game that he wanted us to sing at, because he is such a Phoenix Suns fan that I wanted to give him the option of seeing us at a game that would be significant to him. That was a cool experience.

This era of life with my dad went on for a long time, whenever there weren't other people around. So from about the late nineties and into the new millennium, I really developed and had a great relationship with him.

CHAPTER SEVEN

On The Road Again

SOME of the best times and greatest memories I have of being with dad were the fun adventures we had traveling around the world together on his concert tours. When we were on tour, I would often have to come up with activities for dad and I to do, just to keep us busy when we weren't performing. One of the completely normal and easily incognito things that we could do together was to shop at "Open 24 Hours" places like Walmart stores.

I swear, dad and I have been in just about every Walmart in America, because he just loved shopping there. For anyone who has never been to a Walmart, they are gigantic department stores that carry everything from clothes and shoes, to TVs and CDs, screwdrivers and light bulbs, milk and eggs, and everything in between. Many of them are open all day and all night, and you can stroll through aisle after aisle of every type of merchandise imaginable. Dad loved going there and shopping in every aisle. He just wanted to see everything that was there. He loved doing everyday things like that, which are things that I am sure most celebrities don't do. That really defines part of what dad is about in a nutshell. He is a celebrity on one hand, and at the same time he is just such a simple and uncomplicated guy on the other.

Who on Earth would expect to run into Glen Campbell late at night wandering through a Walmart? No one. This was part of the fun of it. That way he and I could kill time just wandering around like normal people, when we were out touring.

Whenever dad and I were flying somewhere, he was always flying in First Class. I had the option of flying in First Class, or saving money by flying in Coach. I always chose Coach so I had more money to spend on my kids. However, if there were extra seats I would get upgraded. I remember on one particular flight when I was sitting in First Class with dad, they were serving a hot breakfast and I was starving. It was an omelet with ham. At this point in his life dad was following the Messianic Jewish religion. This particular "Jews for Jesus" religion was one that Kim had gotten into, and before long dad had converted to it too. Just like Judaism, they have a strict rule that doesn't allow you to eat pork or shellfish, which they consider to be unclean.

I have always tried to be respectful of these rules whenever I was in his company, but this particular morning I was absolutely starving! So when I didn't think he was looking, I snuck a bite of the ham with my egg. He caught me doing that and said, "Did you just take a bite of that ham?"

I looked at him and said, "Dad I am so hungry."

He took what he was chewing on out of his mouth and he put it smack dab in the middle of my food and said, "Well now eat this."

Needless to say I was done eating right then and there!

There were also some really wonderful memories that I have from this era. Sometime in the late nineties we played at the Red River Opry. My mom and stepdad and both my half-sisters from my mom all came to see the show. While onstage before introducing me to sing with him, dad said, "My first wife Diane is in the audience, and I would just like to say to her: 'Thank you for raising our daughter to be such a kind, loving human being.'" That was *such* an awesome moment in my life as well as my mom's I am sure!

Every year I would allow my kids to take one day off of school to go to the PRO-AM of the Phoenix Open golf tournament. They got to follow their grandpa around the golf course and see other great golfers as well. And my boys loved to golf too, so that was an extra plus. Cal and Shannon came a couple of times with us, and I think Ashley came once.

Anyway, one year dad asked if I wanted to caddy for him. Let me set this story up properly: as much as I enjoyed walking the course and watching him play, up to this point I had never really wanted to go out and try being a golfer's caddy. So I didn't have a grasp of what clubs to use for what distances and so on.

Also, dad was one of the only golfers in the tournament who used a golf cart, so I knew I wouldn't literally be carrying the golf bag, but I was still a little nervous about doing it. Dad did enjoy my company out there, so I said, "OK" as it was another fun thing for us to do as father and daughter.

I had a great time learning the "ins and outs" of caddying that day. I am sure it might have been annoying for some of the other golfers for me to be out there with dad not knowing what I was doing, but dad and I had fun and that in my mind was all that mattered. Those were special moments for me, and of course I would look forward to that the next year and possibly brush up on my caddying skills. However that didn't happen once other people saw an opening for them to get to do the same thing. That would have been Kim's brother-in-law. But to be honest because it was Corey, I wasn't bothered by it as he is one of my favorite people. But because I was the "constant" out there with dad every year it was our special time.

I wonder if other kids of celebrities have dealt with always having to reach out for moments with their parents because of the constant competition with other family, or fans or business contacts? Probably not. I would have to say I'm almost certain of it.

Another thing that we had fun doing amidst some of these events, was singing at karaoke bars. We used to have these really fun karaoke sing-along nights at the Grand Island Hotel with the whole family. Those were just fun, fun nights, where dad could just be something other than the celebrity he was.

On one occasion we went up to either North Dakota or South Dakota for a golf tournament. Basketball star Charles Barkley was also taking part, and we all went out to some bar. It was karaoke night there, and Charles Barkley got up and sang 'Rhinestone Cowboy'. It was the funniest thing to witness, because he was such a bad singer. Dad was just cracking up, so he went up onstage and started singing 'Rhinestone Cowboy' along with Charles just to help him through it. It was so funny, and a great night. I miss those fun and silly times the most.

I don't think that these were things that dad would have done if Kim was there. She wasn't one to let her hair down and allow herself to be that free. I remember some of the fans always saying that he wasn't at all as relaxed if Kim was around.

One of our many nights in the Martini Lounge, which was located in the Grand Island Hotel, I became friends with Jon Murray Stacey. This is the lounge where we would all hang out, dad and I and a lot of our Campbell family singing karaoke. Jon introduced me to his friends Bob and Becky Rushin. They had a beautiful houseboat that Jon invited me join them on, and eventually dad would come with me too. Those were some of the most relaxing days off in Branson. Just hanging out on the boat on Table Rock Lake with them was a lot of fun. They even had a big birthday party on it for me one year and my dad, my aunts and uncles, Jeanne and Don Williams, Jim Barber and his wife, as well as my husband and mother-in-law too. My sister Kelli was dating Steve Ozark at that time, and they even joined us out on the boat that year, as they had come to Branson for a visit. It was such a fun day for all of us.

Dad and I were so blessed to enjoy time with some of the most down-to-earth people while singing in Branson. I truly think dad loved it there for that reason, as he could just relax and people liked his down-to-earth demeanor as well.

Another thing we would do together was that dad and I would spend hours playing gin, especially on long airplane flights. He loves playing that card game. I even remember playing gin with him when I was younger. I would get so frustrated with him though, as he would always "knock".

When you shuffle the cards, and before you deal them, you turn one card up. Whatever the card is, if you have that number of points in your hand or under that number of points, then you can "knock" on the table. So he was always knocking, and I would always say, "Dad, the name of the card game is 'gin', not 'knocking!'" He would do it time and time again, and we would just crack up with laughter.

Finally, after all these years, we had the opportunity to do normal things together. I remember sitting with him in a Laundromat in Reno. We were on tour and we were washing our clothes. The place we were at was called the Rockin' Bee, and it is located in the Reno suburb known as Sparks. Here we were sitting there just like any dad and his daughter, playing gin and waiting for our laundry to be done.

It was a real dive of a Laundromat, so the people who came in there were not looking to run into a Grammy Award-winning country music star. In fact the people who came in there with their dirty laundry paid absolutely zero attention to us. Dad and I got a big kick out of doing normal fun things like that together.

We had finally built a wonderful, wonderful relationship. I could talk to him about anything, and he could talk to me about anything. I learned more about my dad than I had known all of my life. He told me things about his life that I am sure other people have no clue exist. It was like dad had found a friend, who just happened to be his daughter. For this brief period, I had a relationship with dad that I know none of his other adult children had. And I certainly had a relationship with him that none of his public had with him. He wasn't "Glen Campbell" the singing star, he was just my dad.

I think that for dad, I brought a sense of regular everyday normalcy to his life that he didn't always have. I didn't want his money, nor was I drawn to his fame. I just wanted to make up for all of those years in my life when I was growing up, when dad was not around. I didn't need anything from him except his time, and a little piece of his life.

It was never like: "Dad I need money" or "Dad I need this". I had two jobs of my own for that. The only thing that I needed from him was to know that I was part of his life. I didn't know him that well when I was a child, instead I was lucky enough to finally get to know him on a day-to-day basis as an adult, which was something that was always missing.

I loved going on tour with dad during these years. We really got to see a lot of the world, and we also got to hang out a lot together. We were really bonding at this point in our lives. I'll never forget when he said to me one day, "So, this is what it's like to have a relationship with one of your kids?"

And I looked at him and said, "So, this is what it's like to have a relationship with your dad?"

In many ways I wished that this chapter of our lives could have continued just exactly the way it was. Unfortunately, it could not.

CHAPTER EIGHT

By The Time He Got To Scottsdale

THROUGHOUT the years, dad certainly had his eras when his drinking and substance abuse made tabloid headlines. Without a doubt, his affair with Tanya Tucker was the height of this kind of behavior. I also remember an incident when we were in Hawaii in March of 2002, and one night where he got into a big fight with Kim about his excessive drinking. However this really became undeniably evident when dad was arrested on a DUI – driving under the influence of alcohol – charge in 2003. Although this became a shock to the public, I had seen the warning signs. There were several years prior to that, where I saw him overindulging and in total denial about it.

There were a lot of times where I was left thinking, "Dad has really got a major problem, and maybe I should step in and say something."

There were also a couple of instances when I was out on the road with him as part of his concert tours, where I did finally feel compelled to say, "Dad, I think you drink too much." However I mainly kept my thoughts to myself, and I always kept a close eye on him to make sure that he didn't get out of control with it. Dad has always been very strong-willed and opinionated, so that made the idea of starting an argument with him an especially unappealing prospect.

On one particular incident, his business manager Stan was with me and he concurred with my opinion that dad's drinking was getting a bit out of hand. So, we decided to confront him about it.

We were on the road and in a hotel. After the show we would all get together and have a couple of drinks. Dad was drinking and he didn't want to go to bed yet, so he had another one, and another one leads to another one, and by then he had far too many. It wasn't like he was on a self-destructive mission to drink. He simply drank too much.

This particular night, he was so drunk that Stan and I had to put him to bed. We literally had to take his clothes off of him, and we had to get him into the bed, so obviously he had way too much to drink that night.

Stan just happened to be with us since he wasn't usually out on the road with us. We were in dad's room and getting him ready for bed, and still he insisted that he wanted more to drink.

"Go and get me some more wine," dad commanded.

I told him, "Dad, you've had enough."

That's when he got belligerent with us. "Don't either one of you tell me when I've ever had enough of anything!" he insisted. "When you start telling me I've had enough, that's when you are gonna be off of the road! I will do what I want! Nobody ever tells me what I will or won't do. And I will fire you both if you say anything to me!"

As usual, dad had to have the last word. We have had maybe three heated arguments in 20 years, and this was one of them.

After that particular incident it became the norm that in every hotel contract, the mini bars were to be emptied in dad's rooms, or we would take them out of the room altogether. People would also be in the habit of sending champagne or expensive bottles of wine to dad's room trying to be nice and give him a present. We had to put an end to that too. We certainly couldn't have a bottle of champagne waiting there for him anymore, as it just led to trouble.

Without question, we all agreed that it would be best if dad didn't drink at all. Or, should I say, everyone *but* dad agreed to this. Unfortunately, his solution to this problem would be to drink in private, and not tell anyone about it. Dad would get wine and hide it. When we checked into hotels he would hide a bottle behind the toilet. He would also hide bottles inside of the toilet water tank. I would usually find them however. He didn't want anyone to know that he was drinking, so I had to search his hotel rooms to make certain that he wasn't hiding it somewhere.

Up to this point his drinking didn't ever impede his ability to do his show, because he really didn't begin drinking until the show was over, and he was offstage. As time progressed he'd start having a glass of wine before the show. When I confronted him about it he'd say, "I need a glass of wine, it helps me sing better."

But, I think that dad had simply replaced one addiction for another, because he gave up smoking cigarettes, so then he started smoking cigars, and drinking wine goes with smoking cigars. Then when he would go out on the golf course he would drink: golfing and drinking go together. So, he had that kind of scenario going on.

At a certain point, dad went from drinking casually to drinking more excessively. Some people have the ability to consume a lot of alcohol and it doesn't affect them adversely, or change their personality. However, I have to say dad is not a good drinker. In fact, he is an angry kind of drinker, and often he's an argumentative drinker. It all depends on his mood at the time. If he is in a good mood, drinking enhances that. If he is in a bad mood, or if he is mad about something, it only makes it worse.

I remember one particular argument I got into with him during this era. My dad had given me his white Chevy Suburban, and one day my son Jesse asked to borrow it to run down the street to pick up some large object he needed, which wouldn't fit in his car. Jesse was going through a green light and a lady ran her red light and hit the car, smack-dab in the middle of the Suburban, pushing them almost into a canal.

Thank God there was a street light to stop that from happening. Anyway, dad had told me when he gave me the SUV automobile that it was mine only, and that no one else was to drive it.

This episode with the car had happened six or seven months beforehand, but for some reason it continued to irritate dad. One night we were together on the road and at a hotel, when he decided to bring the incident with the Chevy up again. Of course, dad had already had a few glasses of wine when this had occurred. We were sitting downstairs, and the conversation got a little heated.

I said, "Dad, why don't you go up and get some rest, and I'll be up in a minute." So, he did.

I came upstairs a little while later, and when I went in my room there was a copy of *USA Today* lying on the bed, and written in blue Sharpie pen ink were the words: "I told you not to let anyone drive your car."

I found this humorous that dad was so upset that it had resulted in his writing this down, and I went into his room to ask him about it. Dad and I had adjoining rooms, so he came at me pointing his finger at me, and he jabbed me into my chest bone as he said, "I told you not to allow anyone to drive that car!"

He was poking me so hard with his finger that he was hurting me. So, I calmly pushed my adjoining hotel room door shut. I was so upset about this.

It made me recall when Jesse wrecked my car, and how upset I was about the whole incident. First of all, my son could have been badly hurt. And second to that, I knew my dad was going to be so pissed off when I told him about the car accident. However, I didn't know it would last into months later.

I was so angry that I called Bill and told him I was coming off the road the next day, and going home. It started a whole domino effect within dad's road show. Bill's wife was on the road with us, and if I am off the road, Holly is off the road. If Holly is off the road, Bill is off the road, and so on, and so on. We were all traveling on a bus at this point, so if something went wrong with any one of us, it ultimately impacted everyone.

This particular argument with dad was such a big one that I remember that even Kim called me at this point and she asked, "Are you OK?"

I didn't want to blow this episode up, so I simply said to her, "I'm OK, I'm OK. Yeah, we just had a fight." After that, things just went back to normal, as if nothing had happened.

Much to my amazement, at this point, Kim was not fully aware that my dad was drinking a lot after the shows. Kim proclaims that she is very religious to the point that she doesn't drink alcohol at all. Since she had pushed her religious beliefs on my father, she assumed that he was not drinking as well. This was totally unfathomable to me. I could not believe that she could have actually not known that my dad was drinking. For crying out loud! He would go to the golf course, and when he came home you could smell the alcohol. To miss that, you'd have to be naïve, or you simply don't want to know. I found it hard to believe that she could not want to know what was happening. Kim obviously didn't want to face the facts.

To avoid arguing about this with Kim, dad would relegate his drinking to the times when she wasn't around, particularly while we were out on the road. Then there were times on the road when I would question him about how many glasses of wine he had, and dad would say to me, "You better never tell Kim that I'm drinking, because you don't owe her anything. Your allegiance is to me, so you don't ever, ever, say a word to her, because I am your dad, and you don't owe her anything." When it came to issues like this, he was impossible to argue with.

So I said to him, "Well, I'm not gonna lie, so hopefully she never asks me right out if you have been drinking. If she asks me dad, I'm not going to be put in that position where I have to lie to her."

"We'll figure it out if she ever asks you. And you tell me if she comes out and asks you."

Well, the day came when she did finally come out and ask me. I knew that moment would eventually arrive, and she inquired, "Is your dad drinking?"

Fortunately, I'd had enough time to think this out, and I said to her, "Kim, if you have questions like that, you have to ask him. You have to ask my dad yourself. I don't want to get in the middle of your marriage."

I wasn't going to lie to her, but I sure wasn't going to get in the middle of dad's relationship with his wife. This train of thought goes all the way back to Billie when their marriage ended and dad emphatically instructed me, "You're not allowed to ever go back to Billie. She is out of your life. Your allegiance is to your dad!"

Anyway, this routine of dad drinking and hiding it from Kim continued through the nineties and into the next decade. His drinking habits, and his shielding it from Kim, had a direct correlation between his going out to the golf course and drinking too much, and his DUI arrest. This came about just that innocently. However, on that particular day dad made one miscalculated move after another.

It was Monday, November 24, 2003, three days before Thanksgiving. We had just come home from being out on the road, and I knew that Kim was out of town. She was in New York City with her daughter Ashley, and we were all in Phoenix. Ashley was doing something with the Macy's Thanksgiving Day Parade through her school. We had just come in from performing in Minneapolis. The boys – Shannon and Cal – were at home.

Dad went out to a Phoenix golf course with some of his buddies. While they were playing golf, he drank excessively, and got into his car to drive himself home. At an intersection on his way home, while behind the wheel of his BMW, he sideswiped a parked car at the intersection. Fortunately, there was no one in the other car, so no one was hurt in the collision. However, to totally compound the situation, after he hit the other car, he left the scene of the accident. Apparently, he was so confused or horrified by the thought of being recognized or arrested, he simply drove off. That's when it all got complicated.

An eyewitness viewed the whole accident, saw dad leave in his car, and followed him to his house. The witness then proceeded to call the police on a cell phone. Within minutes a police car pulled up to dad and Kim's house, and the officers confronted him with the crime.

In an attempt to shirk any responsibility for the accident, dad yelled into the house, "Shannon, were you out driving my car?" That little ploy of blaming it on his son didn't work out as he planned. The police officers weren't buying it.

In addition to that, since dad appeared intoxicated, he was accused of drunk driving. The police proceeded to arrest him, and subsequently took him to jail in handcuffs. Thankfully, I didn't have to see any of this. That would have been too heartbreaking for me to witness. As it turned out, when his blood was tested for alcohol, he was found to be at 0.15%, when the Arizona legal limit was 0.08%. At the time he had two initial charges against him: extreme DUI, and leaving the scene of an accident.

To make matters even worse, when he was placed in jail, he became argumentative towards the police and "kneed" a sergeant in the thigh, so he was additionally charged with "assaulting an officer". That charge was later dropped, but it certainly made matters worse. Fortunately, I didn't have to witness any of this either. By the time I heard about it, he was in a jail cell already. In other words: By The Time *I* Got To Phoenix and heard about it, he was already behind bars.

According to the press reports, while dad was in the jail he was heard singing his song 'Rhinestone Cowboy' in his cell. When he is confronted with any problems, dad reverts to being very kid-like, so I can just imagine that this is true. There are times when he literally acts like he is a big kid.

Kim was in New York when this all happened, and did not come home to Phoenix. Over the phone she told me that by leaving him in jail, it would teach him a lesson. She wouldn't even take dad's calls for a couple of days.

There was no way in hell that I was going to leave my dad in jail. That simply was not happening. There are some people who would be better off left in jail, but dad is not one of them.

At the time, Mel Schultz was dad's next door neighbor, and I talked to

Mel first, as he is a very good friend of my dad. They both built houses right next to each other in Phoenix. That's how close their friendship was and continues to be.

I said to him, "Mel, I just don't know what to do, and I don't have the cash for dad's bail personally."

Mel and I knew that we had to immediately come up with the cash, so we decided that we should call dad's other friend Earl Jarred. I knew that Earl would probably be able to come up with the cash quickly.

I called Earl, and I said, "Earl, we need to get dad out of jail. He needs our support." He instantly came to our aid.

I went to the other jail, the police substation at the Biltmore, because dad was there before he was transferred to the main jail. When I got there, a female newscaster was there. She was trying to get in to see dad or to get a comment from Mel, Earl or me. I asked her to go away, as we had nothing to say, and to "please leave my dad alone!"

I told her flat out, "You need to just leave. You're not getting anything out of me!" I was really pissed off that she thought she was going to turn this event into a news scoop.

Bail was set at over $100,000, and so Earl went down to the county jail where dad was transferred to get him released. Earl had to wait there for a long time. Finally he called me in the middle of the night, and told me that dad had been successfully bailed out.

As if the headlines in the next day's newspapers weren't bad enough, the press stories were all accompanied by the official police booking photo of dad, which was especially demeaning in itself. Between his disheveled hair and the downward-turned scowl he had on his face, it was an especially shocking sight. The photo depicted dad at his lowest point. It was quite dramatic and truly sad to see.

After we got dad out of jail, my husband and I went to stay with him. When we got there, I found that dad's state of mind was one of total "denial". He wasn't belligerent or anything, because he had spent a night in jail, where he sobered up and sufficiently cooled off. In fact, when he woke up in jail, he claimed that it was quite a shock to him!

My dad is such a sweet, sweet, kind-hearted man. The idea of him waking up in jail is a horrifying vision for me to imagine. This all made for a very bizarre Thanksgiving. It also turned out to be an incredibly humiliating experience for him.

In the meantime, I had married my second husband, Tom, in 2002. I don't know what I would have done without him during this whole ordeal.

While my husband Tom and I were staying with dad that Thursday I cooked us a real Thanksgiving dinner at the house. After dinner we all went next door to Mel's house for dessert. It was just dad and my family.

Stan came over to Phoenix from California, and it was Stan and me who went to the lawyer's office with dad. His ex-wife Sarah even came over to the house to see how he was doing.

The DUI charge was a definite game-changing event in dad's life. Never fond of living in Phoenix, Kim preferred to live near the ocean. So, when Ashley went to Pepperdine University in Malibu, California, this was an opportunity to move.

Kim's sister, with her three kids, had moved to be near them, and I lived in Phoenix with my three kids and granddaughter. Dad had lots of family around and loved it in Phoenix, and they all moved to Malibu. Dad had moved years before from California to Phoenix. Besides his music, his golf was just as important, and he could do that every day in Arizona, all year long. His DUI changed all of that. It altered everything.

Dad was extremely disappointed that the whole DUI charge had transpired. He had seen what excessive drinking could lead to, and he wanted to make certain that it never happened again. He has hardly had anything to drink after that. In fact, I can't come up with one single instance where I recall having seen him with a drink in his hand following that episode. That whole incident was both a humbling and a humiliating occurrence, and it was the beginning of a whole new era in my dad's life.

I have never had a conversation with my dad about the whole DUI incident, because some people are in total denial in thinking that they ever had a problem. In my mind, I think that dad's been struggling for a long time with inner problems and issues that he can't resolve in his mind. I have never been able to really pinpoint what the issue is that haunts him, but he really hasn't been happy.

Dad eventually had to serve 10 days in jail during the year following his drunken car accident. While he was there, a TV news program called *Celebrity Justice* did a segment about him. While serving his sentence for the DUI, he was allowed to bring his own food, and he had his guitar with him at all times.

I said to him, "So, I see you did a concert without me."

He said, "Honey, you should have been here. We had a 'captive' audience."

Sometimes you just have to look on the bright side of things when you are confronted with problems. In this instance, what can I say but, "Well, at least he didn't lose his sense of humor!" That's my dad!

CHAPTER NINE

The Best Of Times

AFTER dad's DUI ordeal was over with, his popularity as a performer was unaffected. In fact from 2003 to 2011, I found that he was just as busy as ever. When I look back on my time in dad's show, I'm happy to say that it was a great 24-year run. I got the best years, and the best relationship with my dad. He and I certainly "hung out" together, especially when we were on the road: in planes, in hotels, in limousines. We had so much fun!

I remember, on flights I would give him crossword puzzles from *People* magazine, while I did the one in *USA Today*. The *People* crosswords are pretty easy. Dad would say, "Hey honey, what's a six-letter word for . . . ?"

And I would say, "Dad, this is my puzzle. That is your puzzle. Figure it out for crying out loud!"

When we were in the airport together, I would buy us every tabloid magazine that there was, because he just loved those magazines. He didn't have to concentrate on anything. He just skimmed through them, and he was entertained for hours.

He is a funny character, my daddy! He would be so irate about spending money on expensive things, but he certainly loved spending it on all of those funny little gadgets he would discover.

Golf clubs were another thing that dad loved to spend money on. He absolutely loved golfing. I was with him through the most intense golfing phase of his life. If I wasn't in the game playing with him, I was riding along with him in the golf cart.

At one point – back when he was married to Sarah – there was even a Glen Campbell Los Angeles Open golf tournament. It went on for four years. It was such a big deal that Jim Beam whiskey even did a special "limited edition" Glen Campbell Los Angeles Open bottle to commemorate it. They are now considered "collector's items" amongst fans. There are Glen Campbell cocktail glasses, tee markers, and all sorts of merchandise that came from these tournaments.

I also remember doing the Phoenix Open Golf Tournament with dad. Vince Gill played it as well, and his second wife Amy Grant was with him. I had a nice conversation with Amy about how complicated it is to have a family with kids from mixed marriages. Amy had kids; Vince had kids. I remember that we agreed that it takes a lot to make it work out smoothly. We both came to the conclusion that if striving to make it all work is your goal, then in the end it *will* all fall into place correctly.

I sang at the AT&T Golf tournament with dad, and I ended up singing background for several of the other performers too, like Vince Gill, John Denver, Charlie Daniels and the Gatlin Brothers. That was a fun event to be at, and that was early in my tenure of singing with my dad.

I recall doing two nights in Charlotte, North Carolina, when dad and I were performing with the symphony there. I would always find things to keep dad busy, whenever we were traveling. Keith Urban was playing at a place across the street from where we were, and dad said, "Let's go over and see Keith Urban."

So we went around to the back of the venue, and there were security guards there of course. They saw us, instantly recognized that it was Glen Campbell, and they all enjoyed talking to him. They called Keith's people, and we waited for someone to come out and get us. We were escorted in there and watched part of Keith's show, and then we went and talked with him for a little bit after the show. It was a great visit.

Another time came when we were up in Canada. We did a show, and there were a lot of other celebrities on the bill with dad. I am not going to mention any names, but there was an incident involving one of the other performers. Now mind you, I have never experienced dad being very rude or should I say "full of himself", so when I experienced it from someone on the staff of another artist this particular evening I was shocked to say the least.

After dad's part in the show was over he was hungry, and he wanted to go and get something to eat. So, we changed our clothes, and we were going to walk to the canteen to get some food, and the other artist who was on the bill with dad happened to have a trailer there. His trailer was next to our trailer and on the way to the canteen.

As we approached, it was this other celebrity's turn to come out of his trailer, to go onstage, and his security guards stopped dad and I and said, "Wait. You can't go."

Dad said, "I'm just going to get something to eat."

The guards said very gruffly, "Well, you will just have to wait. Our artist is about to come out of his trailer, and go onstage."

I said, "Are you serious? You're stopping my dad from walking from his trailer, in front of this trailer to go and get something to eat, because you have to block the way for your artist? Really?" It just floored me. What would it have taken? Two seconds to walk by the trailer, give me a break! I couldn't believe the gall of that!

When Tim McGraw and Faith Hill went on their Soul-to-Soul tour, all of the Campbell kids wanted to go and see them. The boys all wanted to ogle Faith, and all of the girls wanted to go and see Tim.

So dad rented out the entire Phoenix Suns Suite, and the whole family went. I brought all of my kids, and dad and Kim brought all of their kids. It was a really great evening, and the kids just had a blast backstage. The girls all had their picture taken with Tim, and all of the boys had their pictures taken with Faith. They thought it was just the coolest. That was a fun family outing.

When we were doing concert tours, I always traveled with dad and Bill – his tour manager – and the three of us would always travel the day of the show. The band usually traveled the day before the show. After dad and Kim moved to California, I would then fly to California from Phoenix to meet up with dad so that he never had to travel alone.

Dad was always something of a golf snob. He absolutely never liked to golf with any not-so-great golfer. He had no patience for slow or inept players. But, for all of the years that he golfed, he never minded that I wasn't very good at it. I couldn't spend a lot of time on the golf course with him, because I had another job. If I wasn't out on the road singing with dad, I was flying for the airlines. So, when we lived in Branson, I got to golf with dad maybe once or twice a week. He always wanted me out on the golf course with him. Yet, if he was out there on the golf course with someone who wasn't very good, he would be so upset and pissed off. "Why is this person out there?" he would complain, "They can't golf!"

And I would say to him, "But neither can I!"

He said, "That's different, you're my daughter."

He just seriously enjoyed me being out there with him. It mystified me, since I was such a mediocre player. I always thought that was kind of funny, and kind of nice at the same time. In other words, he couldn't tolerate not-so-good golfers, unless it was me, and then it was OK.

Some of my most fun experiences with dad from this era came on our international tours. When we went to Scotland, I wanted to do some research on the Campbell family tree. I kept trying to get over to the Castle Campbell that was there since we are descendents from Argyle, but we always seemed to be two hours away from it. I would also look up historical facts about the Campbell clan in Scotland, and dad would say, "Really? I didn't know that!"

I always found that interesting information to discover. Dad is very much a family-oriented person, so he always found this kind of stuff fascinating.

When we did a tour of England, it would be "one nighters" in little towns, and every night after the show we would travel to the next town. We would get into the car, with Howard Kruger's driver. Howard was from EMI Music, and he was one of the tour's co-promoters. His father was Sir Geoffrey Kruger. We would get in the car at night and travel to the next town we were playing in, and then we would be there all day. That way dad could relax in the hotel during the day.

Meanwhile, Bill and the band would travel during the day before the gig, so we would never be with the band. Dad and I would get in the car the next day. We would sit and chat while being chauffeured to the next town.

We had a great time together in Australia. We went out on all kinds of excursions: we went out walking on the mineral springs, and hung out there. I tried to get dad out of the hotel as much as possible so we could see the sights.

One place we went to was like a "sweat lodge", where we did this one concert. We were dripping with sweat. The place was packed, and there was no air conditioning, so everyone was working up a sweat.

It was an actual "wool shed" where they used to shear the sheep. But it was so hot in there that it felt like a sweat lodge. Oh my God, I remember dad being soaked to the bone after his performance there, but he had such a great time that night. It was a great show!

I would be on flights with dad, and he could not resist spending a lot of time ordering things from the *Sky Mall* catalog that would be on the flights. He would say to me, "Honey, why don't you order this for me. And I want you to order that, and I want that."

I said to him, "Dad, let me use your personal credit card, because I don't want Stan to think I am ordering all of this stuff from *Sky Mall* with the business card that I use for our food and hotel."

He said back to me, "I don't want you ever to think that you have to answer for anything you spend on that credit card, because you are the only person that has one of my credit cards who won't abuse it." So, that made me feel good.

I did have one of his credit cards, and I never abused it in any way. I always gave a complete accounting of what was being spent, and why it was being spent. I have consistently tried to be responsible with money.

For years dad had me buy Christmas presents for my kids from him, because he knew that I would buy sensible things that they needed. He would give me a limit on what I could spend, and I remember shopping our way through *Sky Mall* magazines, and ads on TV.

I swear that dad had a habit of buying nearly everything that was depicted in *Sky Mall*, and he certainly kept himself entertained for hours on flights that way. Another thing that I had to do was to see that dad didn't watch the home-shopping shows on TV for hours on end, or he would instantly say, "Oh, I've got to have that. I want to order one of those right now!"

One day I had an omelet pan that mysteriously arrived in the mail at my house. I couldn't figure out where the heck that came from. Then I saw on the receipt that it was from a TV mail-order company. I never knew what dad was going to order next! He was so funny that way. He just loved to have all of the latest gadgets and contraptions that he saw on TV.

I remember a time when Kim and dad stayed at my house. Of course Kim only sleeps on king size beds, so I would give up our room, and my husband Tom and I slept in our guest bedroom, so that Kim could have our king size bed. Dad always has a permanent ink Sharpie marker with him so he can write things down. The funny thing about dad is that he just grabs whatever it is that is handy to write things on. After they left, I went into my bedroom where they had stayed, and there was a 1-800 toll-free phone number written down on my TV remote control in Sharpie ink.

Obviously, there was something that he wanted to order off of the TV, and the remote control was the only thing he could find to write on. I couldn't believe it!

There was also a box of tissues in there, and on it were written several other telephone numbers that he wanted to call, to order stuff. It was hysterical! He had no forethought about doing this. Whatever was in dad's reach at any given time was instantly pressed into use as his notepad.

On one occasion, one of dad's band members, Kenny, had left his guitar lying around. Well, dad was so used to autographing guitars, that he took a marking pen and wrote "Glen Campbell" on Kenny's personal guitar. That absolutely cracked me up with laughter. I am sure that Kenny didn't feel the same way!

Dad and I did such funny things together. It was early 2000 when I took him for his very first pedicure. I couldn't believe he had never had one. I remember it was in Orange County, California. He decided to have a flower painted on his big toe. I asked him why he would do such a thing. He said he wanted to see how long it took Kim to notice. If my memory serves me right, it took her about a week. I thought it was quite funny and he and I had quite a good laugh about it!

Dad was such a great golfer that it made him quite a perfectionist about the game to say the least. I remember one day he went out golfing with my son Jeremy. Apparently they were out on the course, and Jeremy made a really great shot. And for some reason it really pissed dad off. Jeremy said to him, "Grandpa, look at that! Wow, try and do that! See if you can hit one past this one!"

Well, dad took real offense to that, knowing that he couldn't hit a ball that far anymore. He couldn't hit a ball farther than Jeremy, and he concentrated on that for months. I couldn't believe how mad he was. First of all, dad is really competitive, and the second fact was that he realized that he was aging.

When they came back from golfing, dad would not let it go. He was so mad at Jeremy having shown off that way. I said to him, "Dad, are you kidding me? Jeremy didn't mean anything by saying that. Jeremy adores you. He was just joking around with you."

The next time dad was staying at my house in Phoenix, and I got up one morning, while my husband was still in bed. I came out in the living room, and here he is up and he started in on Jeremy having said what he had said on the golf course. This golfing incident had happened months before.

Dad got into it the minute I entered the living room: "You had better tell your son he had better never disrespect me."

I looked back at him, and already I was angry. With the things that I have seen going on with the other kids in my family, and how they regularly disrespect him, and he never says a thing, because he is married to their mother. I remember thinking, "If he thinks he is going to tell me how to raise my kids, that is not sitting well with me at all."

I love my dad, and I have all the respect in the world for him, but he was not going to talk about my kids – who adore and respect him – over some stupid trivial thing like this.

We walked outside so that we didn't wake up everyone else. We were standing there arguing, and I could not believe we were having this conversation. He said to me, "Well, you'd better not talk to me. I can still take you over my knee and spank you."

Now it was getting comical. Since this was before he had his Alzheimer's diagnosis, maybe this had something to do with it. I argued back at him, "You and what army are going to put me over your knee to accomplish this?"

He was really mad now. So I walked back in the house, trying to get away from him, and I walked back into my bedroom, and he followed me in there, right into the bathroom, yelling and screaming at me over this stupid golf ball incident.

I said to him, "Dad, let's please drop this."

He said, "That's like me telling Kim's dad – Jerry – 'See if you can hit one further than this one . . .'

I argued, "No, that is not anything like you telling Kim's dad, 'Hit one past this one.' You and Jerry are the same age, for crying out loud! And Jerry has never been as good a golfer as you have been! So, no dad, you are not getting away with that comment. That is like comparing apples and oranges!"

Finally, he let it go. That was just how dad was. He would get on one thing that irritated him, and he would stay on it and stay on it, until he beat it into the ground. It was just like when Jesse wrecked my car. We are talking about something that happened eight months ago!

But, dad would just stay on stuff like that, time and time again. The thing that really got me occurred when we were out on the road, and my brother Cal was with us. He came over and sat down at the bar next to me and announced, "You know what? Dad can't stand Jeremy."

I looked at my brother Cal and said, "You are actually looking at me saying to me 'Dad cannot stand his grandson?' Shame on you Cal for even standing there gloating about the possibility of it even being the slightest truth. My son Jeremy: who always went to the airport to pick dad and Kim up all the time, and drove them to the burial site for Madi Schneider, and cleaned their house and absolutely adores his grandpa?" It just sickened me for Cal to be so cruel saying those things.

I was so mad, but I caught my temper right then and there. I was not going to have this argument with him at this time. I knew all about the family politics that were at play at the time, and I was not going to let him "push my buttons". So, I just let it go.

I simply couldn't believe that we were having this conversation at all. That just goes to show you how crazy everything was becoming at the end of my run in dad's show.

How stupid of Cal it was to make a comment like that, just because dad was ranting and raving about this at the house? It really got my goat.

Naturally, in time this all blew over. But for a while it was a really big issue between us, simply because dad would not let it go.

When dad and Kim moved to Malibu, my two boys moved to California with their two boys, and they all four moved over to Oakwood Apartments, that same building that dad owned that I once lived in as well. Since then he sold those apartments, and Kelli, Travis, and Kane were part of that sale, because Billie was a part owner in that as well.

In 2005 we were all in New York City, because the Country Music Awards were being held there, and dad was being honored by being inducted into the Country Music Hall of Fame. While in town we saw the matinee of *Sweeney Todd* on Broadway. Afterwards, Ashley wanted to go to see another Broadway show that night, and I said to her, "That sounds great. How much are the tickets?"

She said, "I think they are around $100 a ticket."

I said, "Well, I really don't have the extra money to go and see another Broadway show."

Naturally, she had her mom's credit card, which essentially dad was paying for. Instead of saying to me, "Well, I will just charge it," she instead said, "Oh, OK, I'll just go by myself then." And that's just what she did.

That — in a nutshell — is the difference between Ashley and me. Knowing that my dad would have been overjoyed to know that he paid for his two girls to go and see a play together, really infuriated me. I know how dad is, and she has a different perspective on him, and the way he thinks.

Another time when Ashley and I were on the road with dad together, we were all going to go to the movies: Ashley, her mom, dad, and I. So, Ashley and I were out for a walk together. She announced, "OK, I am going to buy tickets for my mom and dad and I, and then you can buy your own."

I simply said, "That's fine." So, later on, I mentioned that to Kim. I said, "I am not saying that this actually bothered me, because of whether or not dad is going to pay for my theater ticket or not, it's just the segregated way Ashley handles things that at times is hurtful."

And Kim said to me, "We've always taught our kids that they should never pay for things for 'other people' with their dad's card; they should only pay for themselves."

Well, that was a very telling statement right there.

Ashley would say things to me like, "Take a picture of me and 'my' dad." She wouldn't say, "Take a picture of me and 'dad.'" Instead, she made me feel that we weren't really sisters, and that he wasn't "my dad" too. I have always gotten that feeling from Cal, Shannon and Ashley. It is like they have absolutely no sense that there is anyone else in the family but the three of them. They make me feel like an "outsider" in their minds.

I was never trying to single myself out for the spotlight either onstage, or in dad's personal life. I was always a team player, and I always tried to help everyone out. I tried to help Stan, I tried to help Bill, and I did whatever it was that made dad happy.

I have some great old photographs of the family. There were some great photos amongst them of my dad and his parents. One day dad was over at my house, and he said, "How come I don't have those pictures on my wall?"

And I said, "Those were your pictures, but I found them in the trash. Kim must have been housecleaning".

Dad has always been so simple and uncomplicated. He said to Kim,

"Why can't we have a house like Debby? This house is so easy to get around in."

I just got so tired of being compared to Kim. It made me uncomfortable when he made comments like that. I know that I shouldn't have been uncomfortable. It had nothing to do with anything that I had done, still it always struck me as being slightly upsetting.

Kim and I got along OK. However, there were a lot of straining moments in our relationship. I can get along with anybody, so anyone who is in dad's life, I made a point of getting along with them. First there was Billie, then there was Sarah, and now there was Kim. I am someone who is able to make the best of any situation to be a part of my dad's life, and to have my kids be a part of their grandparents' life. Dad liked having us around. He liked hanging out with my kids. They loved to play golf with their grandpa. It has always been just simple. It has always been "just family".

In the 25 years that Kim was married to my dad, she oversaw the renovating and remodeling of their many houses. When I think back on the homes that dad has lived in with Kim, they were living in a construction zone for 25 years of their 30 years of marriage. First it was renovating the kitchen, then raising the roof of the house for a better view of the mountain, and then selling and building another house only to tear the newly built house apart again. I am *not* exaggerating. Dad did live in a construction zone all those years with people in and out constantly!

I have always tried to include Kim in things during these years. On Kim and dad's 25th wedding anniversary in 2007, of all of dad's children I was the only one that acknowledged it. I remember Kim telling me she was so upset with her kids since they didn't even bother to get them a card.

Since I was the one member of dad's organization who was always getting birthday cakes for everyone in the band and the crew, this extended into my family as well. I wanted to make sure that everyone felt that they were cared about, and that they belonged.

In 2008 we went to Hawaii, Kim and dad and their three kids, and me and two of my kids and granddaughter. My son Jesse lives in New York and couldn't make the trip. Kim's 50th birthday was at this time also so I put together a party for her and Steve Ozark planned the meal. And it was just all of us family.

Things were moving along very smoothly throughout most of the

Me and my dad at my first wedding, held in Great Falls, Montana. Dad flew up from California in a private plane, and on my big day I was surrounded by all of the people I loved, including my mom, my stepdad Jack, my brothers and sisters, and Billie.

This is one of my most cherished pictures of Billie and I, taken in the early 1990s at one of our shows in Orange County, California. She surprised me with this visit. This was around the time she was fighting cancer.

Several generations of Campbells: my brother Dillon, my son Jeremy, dad, me, my daughter Jenny, and my son Jesse. In the front row are Travis' kids Brittany and Trevor. This was taken in Branson. We were celebrating dad's 60th birthday, at a party that I arranged.

Me and dad with my best friend MaryAnne Beaman, after our show in Laughlin, Nevada.

Whenever dad could sing and perform with his brothers and sisters, he leapt at the opportunity. Here he is on stage in Branson with my Aunt Barb and Aunt Sandy.

This was my very first night as the opening act for dad, at the Golden Nugget casino in Las Vegas. We are backstage: my ex-husband Karl, dad, cowboy singing legend Gene Autry and myself.

By singing with dad in his shows I got to meet so many wonderful people, and so many great entertainers. Here is dad and me with country star Kitty Wells and her family, backstage at The Glen Campbell Theater in Branson, Missouri.

In Branson, dad and I would have some of our best times hanging out with the legendary Andy Williams and his incredible family. Here I am with Andy, film star Shirley Jones, and dad, in Andy's dressing room at The Moon River Theater.

In dad's act I would sing all of his duet hits on stage with him. For a long time I also served as his opening act as well. I got to see the world, and best of all, I got to hang out with my dad.

Whenever dad was on the road from 1978 to 2011, I was right there with him, as his duet partner, card-playing buddy and devoted daughter.

Dad played guitar on so many of The Beach Boys' recordings that he was practically a member of the group. When dad and I were singing at The Mohegan Sun casino resort in Connecticut, The Beach Boys with Mike Love were also performing there. After our show we went to see their show, and dad got on stage and sang and played with them.

When dad and I went to see George Jones performing at The Grand Palace Theater in Branson, we got the chance to hang out with him. This photo was taken on George's tour bus.

At Lough Derravaragh in County Westmeath, Ireland, clowning around with dad and his fourth wife, Kim.

When we were on the road, it was up to me to plan activities to keep dad busy when we weren't performing. So of course it all centered around golf. This picture of us was taken in Laughlin, Nevada.

At a certain point I was on the road with dad, and two of my siblings.Left to right: Cal, me, Ashley, dad and Kim.

It wasn't so long ago that I was out on the road with dad, and everything was wonderful. With dad's 20011 disclosure that he was suffering from Alzheimer's Disease, I began to feel feel that the dad I once knew was fading away from me.

decade of the 2000s. Dad was still a popular singing and performing draw, and he was always in demand. For me, it continued to be the best of times. I still had my job with the airlines, and it afforded me the opportunity to tour with dad whenever I wanted. I was able to juggle everything nicely. After all of those growing-up years of not having dad as an active part of my life, we were closer than ever. Then around 2008, piece by piece everything started to change.

CHAPTER TEN

Burning Bridges

IT all seemed to change when Julian Raymond came on the scene. It was around the beginning of 2008, a little before dad started recording his album *Meet Glen Campbell*. This whole project came as a complete and total surprise to me.

Here I thought I was so much in the middle of everything, and then I suddenly realized that I was totally "out of the loop". I didn't hear anything about the plans for the *Meet Glen Campbell* album until the sessions for it were already well underway, with this new guy who was going to produce it: Julian Raymond.

I was absolutely floored by that. All of a sudden I learn that dad is recording a whole new album in Los Angeles, and that Cal, Shannon and Ashley were all going to be on it, and I wasn't even invited to sing on it! Here it was me who had been on the road with dad for all of these years, and I had to hear about it through the grapevine!

I was so upset, when they told me that they were going to let me come over and "try out" for it. What the hell was that about? After all of those years of singing with dad, and I had to audition to see if I was good enough to be on the record that Julian was recording. Really?! I ended up doing some background vocals on the album.

At the very beginning, Julian Raymond was a Glen Campbell fan. He had produced Jakob Dylan and his band the Wallflowers, and some other groups. Apparently, he had met Kim and dad in California, and that is how this all unfolded.

When I mentioned it to dad, of course he had Julian bring me into the project. Kim said that since they were letting me sing on the record, then she thought they had better include my brother Dillon on it as well.

Dillon should have been included also, as he is getting his music career going as well (on his own mind you) and has a really great voice. So why wouldn't any of us kids be asked to sing a backup vocal?

Ultimately, I sang background vocals on the Jackson Browne song 'These Days', and another song. The album was released on August 2008, and received great reviews. It now has the distinction of being the third-to-last of dad's studio albums.

The next thing I knew, Julian started dictating changes in dad's band. Bill McClay told me that Julian said to him that dad's band – Russell, Kenny, Gary, and TJ – didn't look "cool enough" onstage. He thought they needed to start dressing a lot hipper. I thought this was odd, since it was dad's fabulous voice and his musicianship that sold the tickets to the shows. When dad started getting booked on TV talk shows to promote the album, Julian took it upon himself to replace Russell in the band by playing the bass guitar himself.

It wasn't long before my youngest siblings were also incorporated into the band, so that they could be on TV. I asked dad and Kim why they were able to go on the shows with dad and I wasn't? I was the one who had been singing with him all these years.

Unsurprisingly, Kim's response was, "They are trying to break into the music business, and you aren't."

All of a sudden there were all of these signs that I was being viewed as a "second class" part of the organization. When dad played at the Troubadour in Los Angeles, I had to push my way into the show. It wasn't long before Julian moved himself into dad's live shows as well.

In July of 2009 dad was going to be the opening act for Keith Urban at Mandalay Bay in Las Vegas. At the time I was still thinking to myself, "I wonder if I am even going to be a part of this, after everything that I have seen unfold lately."

I was starting to doubt whether or not I was going to be a part of anything anymore. Stan kept reassuring me, "Oh no, you're going to be a part of it. We need the whole family involved in this."

Well, much to my surprise, they kept their promise. Up until the time we left our dressing rooms and headed for the stage.

Although dad's original band was still a part of the show, Cal and Ashley were now starting to be featured as guest stars in the show as well, as well as sporadic appearances from Julian Raymond. Julian was producing dad's albums and helping the kids, so he pretty much had free rein at this point.

But Russell was still at the show helping Bill from behind the scenes and still earning his paycheck. Bill and Russell were great friends and spent a lot of time together on and off the road.

Meanwhile backstage, we were in dad's dressing room getting ready for the show and about seven or eight of Ashley's friends came in and she introduced them to everyone in the room, but just left me standing there with no introductions, so naturally after a moment of feeling uncomfortable I introduced myself. It was the polite thing to do, since Ashley had completely ignored me.

This was just one moment of many that Ashley treated me like that. I would always try to reason with it in my head, as far as the age difference, or she just doesn't see me as her sis. That's OK too. I was not losing sleep over it.

Since it was dad performing as an opening act, it was a shorter show than usual. It was just one night in Vegas, but it was a really cool event. Keith came over to dad's dressing room to say "hello" before we took the stage. I had met Keith on several occasions, but the first time was many years before when Keith had first come to Nashville and "Charles" who worked in dad's Nashville Publishing Office brought him to a private function that we were doing at the OpryLand Hotel. And then of course he would become this huge superstar.

But Keith came backstage and as dad went to shake his hand, he said, "Ladies first", and gave me a hug and said, "Hi Debby, how are you?"

He shook dad's hand, and told him to have a great show and, "Thanks for opening the show."

My son Jeremy was there and I introduced him to Keith as well as everyone else standing there. It was the polite thing to do and of course everyone wanted to meet Keith as well. It was a great night despite the family drama festering in the background.

For years the public who came to see dad's shows, saw he and I as the show, and the fans still thought of us as such a strong family unit. However, backstage it was quite a different story.

That was at the beginning of Cal and Ashley being part of the show, and later that year would be other changes. From that point, I was on the road with Cal, Ashley, and their friends Siggy and Ryan – all the young kids. There was clearly a division between us. I never hung out with them on the road. Ashley was always estranged from me. She also treated me with a distinct sense of cool reserve. Onstage, Ashley and I performed a song together, and dad loved it. As dad's youngest and oldest daughters, Ashley and I had voices that blended well together.

How it was arranged in the show was that dad would introduce me to do a song, then I would introduce Ashley to do a song, and the two of us would sing a song together. The song that Ashley and I did together was Fleetwood Mac's 'Landslide'. This would provide about 10 minutes of the show in which dad could go backstage and have a little break. Then he would come back onstage and Ashley and dad would do something together: the song 'Dueling Banjos'.

After that dad, Ashley and I would do a song as a trio: 'Rolling In My Sweet Baby's Arms'. It was a great show, and this segment was really awesome to see, and a lot of fun to perform onstage.

Anyway, the touring and dad's shows were going great, and then Julian Raymond and Surfdog records came into the picture. Julian and Kim started making all sorts of changes.

It was my sister Ashley who was the first to join us on the road. She had graduated from college and Kim had her come with us to Australia. She played keyboards and some guitar in the show. Kim had made sure all three of her kids with dad took musical lessons when they were growing up. Now they had a platform to display what they had learned.

When we did Australia, the show was constructed so that it was: dad – solo; dad and I; me – solo; Ashley – solo; Ashley and I; dad and Ashley; then all three of us as a trio and then back to dad – solo. Looking back on it, it was a fun and a varied show, and a good tour. Still, there were some definite upsets along the way.

Cal and Shannon weren't on board yet as they were supposedly working in the recording studio with Julian on an album of their own. However, soon after we came back from Australia, I heard that the proposed album wasn't going well, and Cal had reteamed with his old bandmate, Ryan Jarred, to form another band.

It was in 2010 that the incident with the band occurred. That was when it was decided to fire all of the members of dad's band, and to replace them with Cal and his band. I have to say, Cal definitely has every right to be on the road with his dad, especially as he is a very good musician. Kenny, Russell and Gary were simply told when the last show would be. And, this came after 20 something years of devoted service to dad. They stuck with him during some of the most trying times in his life, and they were all shown the door.

I was not at the concert that was to become their final show, which – as I recall – was in Dallas with the Beach Boys. For that particular engagement, dad's part of the show was condensed so I didn't go.

Regardless of who was making the decisions Stan probably figured, "These are Glen's kids, so they have every right to be there."

I remember Sarah telling me that she went to Stan with Dillon, and told him that Dillon wanted to be a part of the shows too, and Stan said to her, "Oh no, we are not trying to have that kind of a 'family' show."

All of a sudden I was informed that dad had a new band that would be with him from now onward. Enter: Cal on drums, and his friends Siggy on bass, and Ryan on guitar. In addition Ashley was now on keyboards and guitar. The only person who was spared the wave of firings was dad's brilliant longtime musical director TJ. Thankfully he was allowed to remain. After all, he had been with dad for over 35 years.

Then, when Cal and Kim and Ashley were suddenly on the road, there were a lot of mixed feelings going on. The show was still being billed as: "Glen Campbell, with Special Guest: Debby Campbell", even though my other siblings were in the band. So I asked if they would please take my name off of the posters and such, as I felt it wasn't fair to Cal and Ashley to not be included on the bill also.

It stayed that way for a while, but along the way I felt very attuned to how the other kids might feel about that. With the *Meet Glen Campbell* album, I remember Kim saying, "Well, Cal is a little upset that Dillon's name was going to be on the album credits as well."

I did two backup tracks for *Meet Glen Campbell*, and ultimately I was on the Jackson Browne cut 'These Days'. I absolutely love that song, and I think it is so in tune with what I think my dad is about. And, I have a whole different perspective on what dad is all about, which is one that no one else quite sees.

When it came time for them to do the album credits, they decided that they were going to list our names from oldest-to-youngest. Naturally that put me on top, but in spite of that, I was always in tune with what everyone else felt about a certain situation.

For me to be on the marquee as: "Glen Campbell, with Special Guest: Debby Campbell" while my other siblings were appearing in the band, just didn't sit right with me. I am always playing the Den Mother, making sure that the band members get a cake on their birthday, and thinking of someone else other than myself. That is just "me" and how I am. I don't know where it comes from, especially amidst all of this crap that I am going through. And, you know what? I am happy being that way.

It wasn't long before the results of all of these changes in dad's band and his show turned out to be less than perfect. Right away I started hearing rumblings behind the scenes about the quality of Ryan's guitar playing.

The very first day they rehearsed, TJ wanted to let Ryan go as he thought he just wasn't a good enough guitar player to be on the road as a member of dad's band *but* he was the lead singer of Instant People so he wasn't going anywhere. And those were Kim's exact words to me. Shannon was eventually welcomed back into the band. He is an accomplished guitar player so he reserved the job.

Suddenly, here I was, traveling on the road with my three siblings who were all around the same age as my own children. Needless to say, a lot of things began to change and shift on the road. I found myself increasingly having to defend my own territory within the show, and within the troupe.

On dad's tour bus, I had slept in the same bunk for 24 years. One night towards the end – this is when Shannon had joined us – I came into the bus to get in my bunk, and there was Shannon asleep in my bed.

When I asked Kim about it, she said, "Do you really have to have the same bunk all the time?"

I was so mad. I ended up sleeping in the back of the bus, in the big couch area – all by myself – that night.

Shannon was the last of the three of them who joined the show. And now he was just going to do what he wanted to do, regardless of everyone. Suddenly it wasn't the Glen Campbell bus, it was the Instant People bus.

The funny thing about my three youngest siblings suddenly being in dad's show, was that they had never really shown any interest in being in his show prior to all of this happening.

As the years progressed, that was going on in my life, and for a brief period I found myself in a bad cycle of drinking. I would drink after every show, just because I felt so lost. Then of course, when you drink too much, you say things that you often regret.

Meanwhile, things started to happen regarding dad's health. He was getting older, and now in his seventies he started to get a bit forgetful. For a couple of years he started using an onstage "teleprompter" so that he could remember his place in the show, or dialogue or the song lyrics. A lot of singers do it, especially if they are learning a new song. However, dad apparently went for some medical tests, and he was diagnosed as having the beginnings of Alzheimer's disease. This was a heartbreaking discovery for all of us.

We did a show in Carmel, Indiana, I believe it was in June. It was with Jimmy Webb too. Dad had a rough night in the show. He was messing up songs and forgetting lyrics and it just wasn't one of his best. The next morning at the airport while I was waiting for my flight home, I was thumbing through the newspaper and came upon the review from the show. It was HORRID! I was so angry I wanted to e-mail or call that reviewer immediately and give him a piece of my mind. But anyway, this concert was probably instrumental in getting dad's Alzheimer's diagnosis confirmed.

In the middle of 2011 he and Kim decided to publicly announce to the world the news about this diagnosis. On top of this, the tour that we were now amidst – with bookings into 2012 and beyond – was suddenly about to become dad's extended "Goodbye Tour". In addition to this, his forthcoming album, *Ghost On The Canvas* (2011), was originally intended to be his final studio album. Unlike the *Meet Glen Campbell* album, the songs on this one all carried with them a theme of finality and mortality. And, it was recorded with several guest musicians including surf guitar star Dick Dale, Brian Setzer from the Stray Cats, Chris Isaak, and Billy Corgan from the Smashing Pumpkins. Produced by Julian Raymond and Howard Willing, it was released on the label Surfdog Records.

To make the announcement to the world, a big article in *People* magazine was planned for its June 22, 2011 issue. When the magazine set the wheels in motion to do this exclusive story on dad's diagnosis, they assigned a reporter to come to dad's Malibu house for the interview.

Kim had said she wanted the kids up at the house in case the reporter wanted to ask them anything, so I flew over to Los Angeles.

There was already high drama going on when I got to the house. Kim was on the phone with Cal trying to talk him into coming to the house so they could possibly get interviewed and get some plugs in for their band. Cal was not coming as he wasn't about getting plugs in. She kept saying, "You need to be here!" But he was not budging. Anyway, the reporter did not come as he needed to reschedule for the next week but they had sent a photographer and a make-up artist to do dad's make-up for the shoot. So I was at the kitchen counter with the make-up lady and dad and she asks me if dad had showered, as he clearly had not shaved and was in a lounging outfit.

I went and told Kim the make-up lady needs her to figure out what dad will be wearing and if he needs to shower, and so on.

The make-up lady said to me, "I can't put make-up on him. He hasn't even had a shower."

I went to Kim and told her the make-up lady needed her attention, and then I went over to my son Jeremy and said, "Honey, take me to airport, I need to go home."

I just could not be around the drama anymore. I told the interviewer, "If you need anything from me, here is my phone number. And if you have to ask me anything, I will be happy to do it over the phone. I am leaving now because I have another job that I need to get to." And then I left.

There was one reporter, named Chris Talbot, at Associated Press. He came to do an interview with dad while we were out on the road. He interviewed Kim, and then he interviewed me as well.

I was so proud of Chris, in that he stuck to his guns and did not say one word about Instant People in the article he wrote. It was about my dad, not Kim's kids' band that she is trying to launch.

Kim was always looking for ways to be with her kids and do things with them on the road. Right before I was let go from the tour, we had been having a conversation about the European tour. And Kim made the comment to me, "And you will be taking turns watching him while we are over there."

Looking back on all of dad's marriages, I can clearly see a pattern. My dad needs to be the number one priority in the lives of all of his wives. Starting with Billie, their marriage fell apart and then his marriage to Sarah crumbled too. Now that Kim was on the road with us, I could see where dad was becoming dependent on her. I feel that this co-dependence was one of the things that has kept them together for so long.

Reviewing our show in Biloxi, Mississippi, on July 18, 2011, what Chris did write for Associated Press was: "Campbell's first performance since announcing he has Alzheimer's, the degenerative brain disease that's slowly robbing him of his memories and abilities, was largely a triumph . . . The good mood is due to the presence of Campbell's family. His wife, Kim, began coming on the road with him three years ago. And his band includes his oldest daughter, Debby Campbell-Cloyd, who sings harmony, and his three youngest children: sons Cal on drums and Shannon on guitar, and daughter Ashley on banjo and keys. All those familiar faces make Campbell feel comfortable . . . As much as Campbell enjoyed being onstage, the few moments he spent in the wings while watching Debby and Ashley sing a cover of Fleetwood Mac's 'Landslide' may have been his favorite. 'I like to hear sister harmonies,' he said in a whisper. 'I don't know what it is. They're amazing. I'm really blessed. It's awesome.'"

The new and evolving arrangement for the show that began in 2010 only lasted about a year or so. For a while I had harbored a sense of dread about the way things were going in dad's show, and in August and the beginning of September it all started unraveling at a quicker pace.

I remember a show that we did in St. Louis, and I was standing backstage with dad. We had this guy by the name of Johnny – who we called J.O. – who was responsible for printing the set list, running the teleprompter, setting up the stage, and helping Bill with whatever needed to be done. He had the set list for that night's show, and I looked at it, and I wasn't on it, and Ashley wasn't on it either. There was no "dad and I", there was no "Ashley and I", it was all dad.

By now, Cal's band, Instant People, was the opening act for dad. One of the things we had to do during the Instant People segment of the show was to keep dad out of earshot from the stage. This is because whenever he hears loud music before a show, he doesn't like to hear a band that's loud. And of course Instant People was a loud band: they're kids and that's how they play music.

So, I was backstage with dad, and he said to me, "So, you ready to go out there and sing some duets?"

And I said to him, "Dad, I was looking at the set list, and we aren't doing any duets tonight."

He said, "What do you mean, 'We aren't doing any duets tonight?'"

I said, "Well, here it is. I'm not even on here. I'm not singing, Ashley's not singing, and we're not singing."

"Well, who made that set list?"

"I don't know dad," I said.

Of course my instincts told me that the answer to the question was, "Probably your darling wife," but I couldn't say it.

For me, that was the show before the last one. I was quite upset not to be included in the set list. I phoned Stan immediately. I always thought that Stan was "in my corner", I thought that he was like my uncle, I thought he was family. But by now, I was starting to see how it all was going to play out.

I am sure that Stan was – in his own mind – doing what he had to do. He had to look out for his job, so he did what he was told to do.

I said to Stan, "That is it! I am quitting! I can't handle any more of this."

He said to me, "Now, now, just calm down."

The next day I talked to Kim about it. I said to her, "To get a show's set list 10 minutes before the show starts, and to find out that I am not even on the show: what kind of nonsense is that?"

"Oh, Debby, come on. Why can't you just 'go with the flow'?"

"I know all about 'going with the flow' Kim, but they've known about this set list all day long, and I am reading it 10 minutes before show time? What kind of crap is that? That is pretty downright disrespectful, if you ask me."

I took a deep breath, and I said to her, "Well, now that I am looking at it, I guess I am not needed here anymore."

And she said without hesitation, "Well no, you're really not, but we love you, so we want you with us on the road." She also said that Surfdog needed the album promoted so they didn't want us kids taking up space in the show, where Dad could be doing songs from the album only, along with the greatest hits.

So then the next night we were doing a show in Forrest City, Arkansas, and of course all of the relatives were coming in to see it. And, they were also filming a documentary at this time, so of course all of the aunts were going to be a part of the show this time. They decided to redo the show tonight to make it so that all of the family members could sing with dad. So, suddenly I am back in the show doing a song with dad. The aunts are doing a song, and Uncle Gerald is doing a song; everybody's doing a song. Well, that was to be my last show.

Our usual routine was: we would get off the road, we would come home and we would have a couple of days at home before we would take off again. Well, this time, I went home, and Stan called and said to me, "It's over. You're done."

I said, "What do you mean?"

He said, "They had a meeting today, and they don't need you on the road anymore."

I was stunned, and I was upset. But, I have to admit that I had seen it all slowly unfolding for over a year, so I should have expected it. Still, it hurt – a lot. This took place on September 18, 2011.

TJ called me, and he said, "I couldn't do anything about it. I need this job. This job is all I have, and had I gone against anyone in this meeting, then I might lose my job, and I need this job."

I told him, "I understand."

It made me feel real good that TJ actually called me to tell me that. Even Siggy, my sister's boyfriend, texted me to said, "Deb: I'm so sorry to hear what happened. I know what that feels like."

I thought to myself, "No, you don't know what that feels like. You only know what it's like to be a band member who got fired from a band. I feel like a daughter who has been fired from her family."

While all of this was going on, there were all of these camera crews following dad around, working on a documentary about his Alzheimer's and how his entire family is rallying around him to help him. Well, I had to ask myself, "What are they classifying as family? Do they just mean dad's family with Kim, or does this encompass the rest of us as well?"

Before I got fired, we were backstage at Forrest City, Arkansas, and a fan was talking to Kim and I, and she started talking about losing her parents to Alzheimer's disease. She said to Kim, "I hate to tell you this Kim, but with Alzheimer's patients, as it gets worse, they remember the people they have known longer in their lives than they do the people then have known in recent years. He is going to remember Debby longer than he will remember you and Ashley."

That was a prophetic statement, if ever I had heard one! Within a week I was going to suddenly lose my job and no longer be an active part of my dad's life? I should have seen this coming! I was absolutely horrified as I watched Ashley take my place in the show, after all these years. Suddenly it is Ashley who is at the forefront of dad's show.

Now, I have to say that Ashley has every right to be there, as Cal and Shannon have every right to be there. However, I have a right to be there too. This was even more hurtful and even more important to me because of this was now being billed as dad's big "Goodbye Tour". I needed to be with my dad even more than ever, because eventually, he is not going to know who I am.

For 24 years I had been a key part of my dad's concert show. Now it was suddenly all over. The very first song that I had ever sung with dad onstage was his hit 'Burning Bridges'. Now it was time to start burning some bridges of my own.

CHAPTER ELEVEN

Unconditional Love

IN the days following my firing from dad's show, I found myself so upset that I started writing my thoughts down so that I could sort out all of my feelings. It was a good way to make decisions about my new and redefined role in my dad's life.

JOURNAL ENTRY / October 1, 2011

This is the conversation that I had with my dad today for the first time since I was let go from G.C. Organization. I have heard nothing since September 18 when I was let go by dad's business manager, Stan Schneider. I called the Silver Legacy, where dad is performing tonight. My dad seemed extremely tired today.

He said "Hello" and asked me how my husband was. He told me to tell Tom "Hello", and I asked him about the current events that were going on, and why I had been fired.

He said, "Honey, since you don't play an instrument, and we did only sing two songs together in the show, this is strictly a business decision."

I said, "OK, you are telling me that it was fine for 24 years when I only sang two songs in the show and took care of you on the road, but now because I don't play a musical instrument, and that my three siblings do, then I need to be cut out for business purposes?"

"I'll look into it," he said.

"Please don't look into it," I told him. "Because there is no way I would ever consider going out on the road again in such a toxic environment!"

I told him that I wanted him to do a great show. I then told him that "family" and "business" were two separate entities in my book, and that was the end of this conversation.

On October 22, 2011 I flew from Phoenix to London, with my son Jeremy, to see what was being billed as my dad's "Goodbye Concert" in a city which he has always regarded as one of his favorite places to play. Dad has always loved London, and it has consistently loved him back.

I had mixed feelings about going to the concert after I had been "let go" from the show. However, before I was fired I had already cleared my airline schedule to make the tour. Some of my friends that had family in England and Ireland had purchased tickets for shows thinking that I would be performing. My friend Steve had actually purchased 10 tickets for dad's concert at the Royal Festival Hall. His friend's father had Alzheimer's and had grown up on my dad's music. So they were bringing his dad to share this great musical memory. Ultimately, I decided to put my own hurt feelings aside and to go ahead and make the journey, as I had so many wonderful memories of London from my childhood with dad as well, so I made plans to go with Jeremy.

It had been a month since being fired from his band, after more than 20 years of always being there for him onstage. For me, the past month had been wildly emotional. At first I was dealing with feelings of anger and indignation. "How could I be fired from dad's act at a time like this?" I asked myself.

Pretty soon my feelings morphed from shock and amazement into pain and hurt. Knowing that dad's recent diagnosis of having Alzheimer's disease meant he would inevitably descend into a fog of forgetfulness over the coming years, and that I was being removed from his day-to-day world, deeply saddened and depressed me. "How could I be written out, at a time when dad really needs me?" I kept asking myself.

As I got off of the plane and I walked through London's Heathrow Airport, I found that I was in a completely different place, emotionally. I had arrived in England with a new perspective, one I can best describe as "centered but resigned". I was calm and accepting of what my relationship with my father was going to be like from this point forward.

Although I was centered, I still had a lot of anxiety about seeing dad. Would he be happy that I flew in to see him? Would he be upset, or con-fused, or unaware of all of the family drama that was in the process of unfolding? I was also concerned about myself, and about how I would be left feeling after the weekend was over.

Even with certain things resolved in my mind, my visit was surrounded by a sort of cloud of sadness. When I arrived at the Royal Festival Hall that evening, I wasn't sure what to expect, or where I would be sitting for the concert. Steve actually had a seat for me and Jeremy if we wanted to use them, but I was too nervous to sit out in the audience.

I ended up seeing the entire show from backstage, in the wings of the theater, which was a perfect vantage point. When I saw dad before the show, he was genuinely glad to see me, and he even asked me to sing a duet with him during the show.

"That is so sweet of you," I said to him, "I would love to sing with you tonight."

I just figured at the time, "If he remembers, I will gladly go out onstage with him and perform one of our duets. If he doesn't, that's not a big deal to me."

However, when dad was onstage, and the time slot in the show for the duet came around, he had already forgotten that he had asked me to sing with him. The moment simply came and passed without a word. That was how progressed his memory loss had become.

Imagine my surprise – "not!" – when Ashley and Shannon sang a song together, which became their introduction to their new band Victoria Ghost.

I just let it go. When he forgot about it, I simply chalked it up to his present condition. Minutes after he says things, he simply forgets all about it. He has Alzheimer's disease, so what can I do or say? When he came off of the stage, I never said anything to him about the missing duet.

Backstage before, after, and during the show, there was a sense of oddness in the air. It wasn't the same easy-going and friendly atmosphere that I was used to from the past.

It was particularly interesting to be with everyone, especially after the shocking story about dad that had appeared in *The National Enquirer* that week. The tabloid article was entitled "Battle Over Glen Campbell's Fortune", and it spoke about the various members of the family being at each other's throats. It also mentioned my recent firing in the piece.

When I saw Stan backstage, he looked at me and said, "Boy you have a lot of nerve showing up here."

And I looked back at him not understanding him questioning me.

He said, "*The National Enquirer* article."

I said, "Do you actually think I wrote this article Stan? First off, the article says dad 'is worth $50 million?' Really? That's news to me. And in the article I have been classified as 'dad's backup singer?' I was always 'a featured artist.'"

It seemed that everyone thought that I had sold the story to *The National Enquirer*, and then still had the nerve to show up at the concert. Not only did I not sell the story to the tabloids, I did not care one bit what anyone thought or said to me.

Now, up to this point Kim had been avoiding me, but she had to rush out to watch Instant People who were opening the show. This is what she did every night while someone else stayed backstage with dad. It was Steve Ozark's assignment to look after dad.

After the show was over, I brought my friend Steve Rio backstage with all of his guests and they met dad and had their pictures taken. I said my "goodbyes" to dad and he was dumbfounded as to where I was going. I told him that Jeremy and I would be flying home the next day. So I then went to find Pablo, our driver from our previous tour. When I found out we would be returning for another tour I had let him know so he could work on it from his end, by securing the driving spot for us once again. We had become good friends on that previous tour.

And I wanted to say "goodbye" to Howard of course. Howard Krueger is the son of Sir Jeffrey Krueger who was the first person to bring dad to England. And they remained great friends all these years and for many more tours. Howard was around my age and we were friends, and he took over for his dad in the latter years and he had co-promoted our European Tour. And it was Howard's driver who had driven us for many other tours.

I wanted to say "goodbye" to the other crew members, especially Denzel. I had been so happy to see him. We had hung out on a tour in the past and toured some castles together. I remember a castle in Norwich, England, that we toured and I learned a lot about the Anglos and Saxons that year and their different styles of building. Denzel said he had only signed up to be a part of this tour because he thought I would be there.

So I had not only come to see dad and get the much needed closure, but also to say "goodbye" to friends I had made along the way.

I felt that by going to London to see my dad, it was going to give me a sense of closure. And indeed it did. The shock of being fired from dad's show after 24 years had begun to wear off. Although I wasn't happy with the current situation, I was at peace with it.

As I drove to Heathrow Airport that day after the London concert, a sea of sad, touching, and loving memories came flooding over me. I was taken aback by the many recollections of my father that I had from years ago when we were both in England. I thought about how he would send a limousine to pick me up when I was a teenager at school there. I recalled the day in London when we were mobbed by fans. And I remembered how proud I was to sing duets with him on the British stage. I was content knowing that these were my memories, and no one could take them away from me.

As I flew back to the United States, I felt good. I felt like a gigantic weight had been lifted from my mind, and that I was ready to get on with my life again. I decided that I was "all good" with whatever happens from this point forward.

So starts the next phase to my life, and the next phase in the continuing saga of my relationship with my father. On one hand, it is a sad ending to a huge chapter of my life. I knew that my life with my dad would never be quite the same. Maybe the word "bittersweet" is the appropriate one in this situation. It was like I had come full circle.

JOURNAL ENTRY / November 2, 2011

I watched dad's new music video last night, which was mainly footage of just dad and his band. What I love about the G.C. Organization is that there is no loyalty. TJ has been with dad for over 35 years, and doesn't even make the video.

My emotions are so up and down these days, that if I could say something to my dad at this very moment, I would tell him that I am very disappointed that he didn't stick up for me to his wife, or to Stan, to Bill, to Julian Raymond, and the record company. I would say to him: "Aren't you the boss of your own life as to your tour and who goes on tour with you? No. I toured with you for 24 years, city-to-city, walking street-after-street, golf course–after–golf course, breakfast/lunch/dinners, venue-to-venue, making sure that you – dad – the star of the show, had everything you needed, while your loving wife stayed home with your three children, and I am cut out of the tour. Are you kidding me dad? Steve Ozark, who had a relationship with your second wife, with your daughter

Kelli, and is now traveling with you looking out for you, and I am not there 'for budgeting reasons?' That's the kind of 'loyalty' that exists in this family and organization?!"

These are just some of the ramblings of a depressed girl: me! It is amazing to me, the way that things have taken a turn for the worse.

Once I was let go from the performances, my need and desire to see my father did not subside. I didn't work with him any longer, but I still needed to spend time with him. To accomplish this I would attend some of his shows when I could fit it in my schedule. One of the first shows I attended after my firing and after the London gig was in Louisiana in 2012.

I will never forget the disenfranchised way I felt that night. Since I was not part of the entourage, I no longer had a valid backstage pass to get into the shows, or to have any backstage access to dad. I didn't want to see the show, since I found it too upsetting to watch anymore. I just wanted to see my dad. All of the relatives were there that night, as they had come in from nearby Arkansas. So, I basically wanted to see the whole family, and see my dad at the same time.

So, after the show was over, I went to the backstage door, and there were already a lot of dad's fans waiting, and I said to the security guard, "I am Glen's daughter, and I would like to go backstage."

He said, "Let me radio back there, and see if I can let you in."

After a few minutes, it was all cleared up, and I went backstage. I saw dad, and I fortunately didn't see Kim.

One by one each family member took their turns hugging on dad. It was a surreal moment, as in the past I was the one standing with dad, saying "Hello" to all, and getting hugs and kisses. Now, I was just like the rest of the family, waiting my turn to hug and kiss the legend. I waited for an opportunity to get a picture with dad and my sister Kelli.

I got to hug him. Well, when I hugged him, he just held onto me so long and so tight. He was just so obviously happy to see me.

He said to me, "Oh my God, I am so tired."

I didn't get to talk to him much that night. We had very little quality time at all.

As I waited Kim came in a door, and thankfully she didn't see me. I quietly slipped out of the door and waited for my sister and cousins, and we spent the rest of the night laughing and gambling.

The next morning my flight was an early one, so I texted the bus driver and asked her what time they would all be heading out. She said she hadn't heard.

When I got Bill on the phone, he said they were departing at 9:00, which was in a half hour.

I went downstairs and my friend Bob Krepps – who is a longtime friend of the family – was going to take me to the airport. Kim came down and she sheepishly walked by me, hugging the wall all the way to the bus, with her head held down. Clearly she didn't want to make eye contact with me.

I was standing and saying goodbye to Cal, while showing him pictures of my two-year-old grandson playing drums. Ashley came over and said, "Hi Sis", and tried to give me a hug. I looked at her and was in utter shock. She has never shown any sort of affection towards me in all these years. I was so taken aback by this. Why in the world was she reaching out to me now? And I was tired of all the pretense. So, needless to say I wasn't friendly toward her at all. She walked away, not knowing what to say.

Then dad finally came out to give me a hug, and he said hello to Bob.

Well, the next thing I knew, Ashley walked back up to me, and demanded to know, "Why are you pushing me away in front of dad?"

So, now I found myself having this kind of agitated conversation with her. And dad started to act a little agitated with whatever it was that had transpired between his youngest and his oldest daughters.

I just said to Ashley, "I really don't want to go into it right now."

That was in February of 2012, and then they came to Phoenix in March to perform. I know all of the people who work for the Phoenix theatre where dad performed, so I didn't have to rely on anyone from dad's organization to give me backstage access the night he was performing there.

I was with my family, and we all went backstage to the dressing room. I went up to Ashley, and I said, "Ash, I have to tell you, I was kinda taken aback with you in Louisiana, that you would even want to hug me. In all of these years, you have never reached out to me. You've never hugged me. You've never introduced me to any of your friends as being your sister. The most interaction we have had is you walking over to me and saying, 'Will you take a picture of me and my brothers?' You have managed to always segregate whatever we are to each other. Now that I am no longer a part of dad's show, or the 'inner circle,' you suddenly want to hug me and talk to me? I am just kinda having a hard time dealing with that. But, that being said, I do love you, and I have always loved you, and I only wish the best for you."

That was all I had to say to her. I gave her a hug, and to this day, that is the last that I have had to say to her. We have never had another conversation. There just comes a time in your life when you have to decide what people you want to spend the rest of your life with, and what people you want to say "goodbye" to. I was just "done" with that whole side of the family.

Probably, if dad's frame of mind was even remotely "OK" now, I might be more amenable to "making nice" with everyone for his sake, or I might have a different attitude. Dad is still my dad, and I still want to be around him.

It is such a sad shame, because I know now that dad's mental state is not going to improve. Here I find myself in a space where on one hand I want to spend more time with him, but because of what is going on in California, I don't want to be around that drama.

I remember, after I got fired, on one occasion I called Kim's stepmother.

Of course they had no clue that this had transpired. I would have thought they would known that by the time I called them. And Kim's stepmom's only comment to me was, "Well, I think you had 'a good run.'"

And I thought, "How does one have 'a good run' in the life of one of your parents?" And, how does one say that to someone? "You had 'a good run' with your dad?" I just didn't get it.

"Well you just had 'a good run' didn't you?" I was blown away to hear that. Right after that call I took her number out of my cell phone.

One part of this whole chain of events that really, really upset me came when dad played Phoenix in March of 2012. That was the first time I had seen Kim's sister Pam, since all of this "firing" business went down. If I had not got gone up and hugged her, she wouldn't have said a word to me. I remember, she looked at me like, "Who are you to hug me?" She was actually startled that I would be warm towards her. I didn't think that there was anything awkward between us at all, but I could see that everyone had since chosen sides. They were either on Kim's side, or on my side.

At one point I had heard that Kim had thought about moving dad to Nashville. Well, it didn't happen. My dad absolutely put his foot down, and that was the end of that. There was no way he was moving to Nash-ville. Then when dad was diagnosed with Alzheimer's, the country music world came out to embrace him.

What Kim has created now is a situation where she is the one looking after dad's needs. He always wants to know where Kim is, the devoted wife, and he is dependent on her. Now he doesn't want to know where anyone else in the world is at any given moment, he just wants to know: "Where is Kim?" Part of it is because of the disease – which I understand.

Ever since September 18, 2011, I have been struggling to put all of this in order in my head. Before she suddenly started coming out on the road with us she was busy doing her thing. I was out there at his golf tourna-ments and on the road with him, taking care of him.

After she started coming on the road with us, I still had to carry extra things for dad as she seemed to never pack everything he needed. She would come to my room and ask if I had a hair brush, or an extra tooth-brush, or reading glasses, or socks as she always seemed to forget some-thing for dad. And she would try to get me to iron dad's shirts too. Mind you, I did do all these things for dad when it was just me and him on the road.

Suddenly I found myself taking care of both of them.

Kim had tried for years to get me to move to Malibu, so that I could live with them and help her with dad. But that was before the Alzheimer's diagnosis.

However, I just didn't see myself commuting back and forth to and from Phoenix, just to help them out. I have my airline job, and I have my own bills to pay. I had my own family to take care of too.

I also felt: "What I don't have to see, won't bother me." So I could never see myself moving over there, because when I would go over there to visit, some of the stuff that was going on around the house would have made me nuts in no time.

That is part of the reason why I so valued my time around my dad on the road. I could spend quality time with him, and not have to deal with all of the things that went on over in Malibu! Slowly I started to concen-trate on my life again.

CHAPTER TWELVE

These Days

AFTER I left dad's show in 2011, and he continued on the road with his "Goodbye" concert tour, longtime fans naturally expected me to be appearing in the show, as I had done for the past 24 years. As the shows unfolded, it became clear to them that I was no longer part of the show. Almost immediately I began getting e-mails and letters from fans who were disappointed that I was not part of dad's troupe anymore, and that my segment was missing from the show.

One of the first ones read:

FAN LETTER #1 / CIRCA 2011.

When we got to Philly, and I was told that you would no longer be there as part of the show, it was very upsetting. It was like a punch in the stomach. It is very upsetting the way that things have turned out. First the guys, and now you. It's just not the same anymore. And I am sure that it is very disconcerting for your dad to have to deal with all of these changes, in his condition. Thank you for your kindness throughout the years, and my mother and I wish you all the best. You are in our thoughts.

FAN LETTER #2 / CIRCA 2012.

First of all, whatever conversation you had with your dad, had an impact on the show on Saturday night. He was different. The dad you know and love, is the same beautiful human being I have known and loved since I was a teenager, and his soul is real and so is his heart. Forgiveness will prevail. I just know that it will. Stay with it, and don't despair. He loves you, and he is not stupid or incompetent. Please let me know if you are in Orange County in the future, as I would love to see you. Please don't despair.

These are just two of dad's fans, and they see through the whole way that things are unfolding. Some people have written: "How can Debby desert her father when he needs her the most?" and "How can Debby quit when he has Alzheimer's?"

Just because I haven't publicly said anything, they all think that I have deserted my dad in his time of need. Nothing can be further from the truth.

JOURNAL ENTRY / CIRCA 2012

A secure feeling can be taken away in a moment's notice. I have had a few close friends go through this similar situation. When their dads remarried, they became "the nonexistent child". I felt so sad at their loss, as I had been so close to dad for so many years. I mean after all: this was my third stepmom and I had fought all these years to maintain my relationship with dad. Wow, just writing that word – "fought" – was meaningful. Should we ever have to "fight" to have a relationship with our parents?

So, now let's talk about my sister Ashley. She has never really reached out to me. After all I am two years older than her mother. But we merely existed in each other's lives, and the same with Shannon.

My heartstrings however do feel a tug when I think about Cal. He has a sweet softness about him.

JOURNAL ENTRY: February 1, 2012

I called Stan today as I felt I deserved to go to the Grammys to see my dad's performance, which is surely to be his last Grammys performance. And of course, he "hmmm-hawed" around, giving me all of the excuses. He said, "Even Sandy Brokow can't get a ticket." Sandy was dad's publicist all these years.

I said, "Stan, with all due respect to Sandy, I am Glen's daughter."

Stan said, "There will probably be tickets available for the Grammy Museum Ceremony on February 6." I knew I would have a hard time getting rid of my airline trip for that day, but I told Jeremy to see if he could go. He e-mailed Kim, and of course he was told there were no more tickets for that day.

If dad knew and could comprehend what was going on around him, he would be so angry!

Here they can plunk dad in front of the teleprompter, and do a whole show of all of his hits, but they can't give him something on paper, with his glasses on to read, accepting his Lifetime Grammy Achievement Award.

I was astonished when Kim said to him, "Well, don't you want to accept this award on behalf of your four kids, Cal, Shannon, Ashley and Dillon?"

Someone could have written something out for dad to read. He could have read it himself.

When I think of how my son Jeremy went up and cleaned their house every week. Kim was paying someone else, and Jeremy didn't mind the hard work, so why not pay the grandson to do it, since no one living there would help out? And now, she can't even get a ticket for him to watch his grandpa receive his Lifetime Achievement Grammy? Meanwhile, dad's business manager and all of his family got tickets to go! It is absolutely astonishing to me.

FAN LETTER #3 / CIRCA 2012:

It goes without saying, this is a very special week for your father and all the Glen Campbell fans. Receiving a Lifetime Grammy Award is nothing short of spectacular. It's just awesome. And if I could present you with a 'Lifetime Devoted Daughter Award' this week, I would certainly do so. You are as much a part of the award that your dad is receiving Sunday, as any Campbell family member, and as an ardent supporter of his music and career for many years, your contributions and standing by him for these years as his duet partner and member of the cast of the show, should make you very, very proud. Not a moment will go by watching all these wonderful tributes and the Grammys, that we won't think of you, and know how much you did for your father and his fans, for many, many years.

JOURNAL ENTRY / February 16, 2012

Today as I sit in the back of this airplane on my way back home from Washington DC to Phoenix, my mind is always wandering, reflecting on what's happening in my dad's life. I had nothing to gain by being a part of my dad's life, except being his daughter, and being there with him. I wasn't making a big monetary gain out of all of this. I really felt bad for all of the old band members. I even felt bad for Russell, and I didn't even have a close relationship with him. For some reason, Russell and I just never became close. Even though in Branson at all the theaters we played at, if there was a birthday of a band member, I organized birthday cakes, and I orchestrated birthday parties for each band member, to make them feel special. I took the school mom role in these instances. Here we all were away from our families, and I wanted to make them feel special.

I haven't written anything down in a while. Basically, I have been trying to push everything out of my mind. I was thinking of flying to Fayetteville for dad's show April 27 and 28. I was thinking about going, but I am always a wreck for a couple of weeks after seeing dad. After I see him, I just fall apart thinking about everything that has happened. So, I am opting out of going to Fayetteville, just to stay close to people who I love, who love me, and who I need to be around. I don't want to be around Kim anymore, and what she represents. But I still want to go and be around my aunts and all of the family. Dad doesn't seem to realize what is going on around him.

JOURNAL ENTRY / March 8, 2012

I had a wonderful conversation with my ex-sister-in-law, Andrea, today. I am glad we talked as she was very helpful in sorting out a lot of my feelings. I am so proud to hear that my niece Brittany expressed her feelings of dismay to Kim, about being left out of the Grammy festivities. My siblings – from Kim and dad – had their friends there with them at the Grammy event, but the rest of the family were not there. Here I was – the daughter, my son Jeremy – the grandson, and Brittany and Trevor – the grandchildren, and we all missed this milestone event in dad's life.

Andrea has, for all these years, done the same as I have. We both only wanted to be a part of his life, and for our children to have their grandparent, so we tried our hand at "playing nice" with others – so to speak. I have never been one to stand up to Kim when faced with some things that I didn't like, as I didn't want to upset the apple cart. I just wanted my dad in my life—no matter what, but now I don't care what Kim thinks, nor do I care what anyone around dad thinks for that matter. I seem to be on the outside looking in. Even though I am experiencing these feelings of relief, I am sad, as dad is not in my life anymore.

Andrea suggested I make nice with Kim for the sake of our family, but I am really having a hard time with this.

I don't really know if I could be around any of my three youngest siblings anymore. And I definitely couldn't care less about what any of the G.C. Organization thinks either. This "big time show-biz" lifestyle really sucks!

I miss my dad, and the many wonderful conversations we used to share. And I do know those days are gone as dad forgets one moment to the next.

JOURNAL ENTRY / March 12, 2012

I called dad today and he sounded sooo tired. We didn't talk about much. He said he had been golfing and they were just having him go here and there.

So, that was the extent of our conversation. He kept asking how I was, and I told him that I was "fine". And, I told him, "I love you", and he said the same, and that was it.

Our brief dialogue made me sad, and made me realize how much I truly miss our regular talks.

JOURNAL ENTRY / April 22, 2012

Today is my dad's 76th birthday. It is very sad for me. I called and I talked to him. What a difference a year makes in a life. Just a year ago we were there, opening all of his birthday cards. Fans had sent all of these cards to him. They thought, "Let's do something very special for him for his 75th birthday." So, instead of writing messages to him on the computer, and sitting with dad and letting him read everything that the fans had written, we had them send cards in the mail, and that was so special for them to do that, and dad was so excited to open all of these cards.

I remember Ashley making a comment to someone that dad had some really crazy fans that follow him around the world, buying tickets to every show all the time, and I wanted to say to her in front of all those people, "Well, let's hope Ash, that you'll be able to win over fans like that who want to go every show you ever do!" But, of course, I kept my mouth shut once again.

I sat there watching dad open all of these birthday cards from all over the world. It was very special indeed. His 75th birthday was a great milestone for him, and it was such a happy time. All my kids were there, and even my ex-husband was there. I was so happy to be there in Malibu with him.

However, by the time his 76th birthday rolled around, in 2012, I found that I was no longer in his life anymore. What a sad difference this past year made.

Kim had been astonished that I would think nothing of having my ex-husband Karl there for dad's birthday in 2011. It just illustrates how different she and I are.

I remember Kim saying to me that day, "That's very gracious of you, that it doesn't bother you to have your ex-husband, Karl, here."

I said to her, "Kim, it doesn't bother me because my main passion in life is that my kids are happy, and that they are at peace with themselves, and that they can have a happy, functional life. That means that they probably need the support of both of their parents in their life. So, they need something from their dad. Here we are: all in the same state – in California – even though Karl lives in Missouri, and we are all under the same roof; so why not? It doesn't bother me. It was up to you. Does it bother you that my ex-husband comes to dad's birthday party? I don't care, Karl doesn't care. So, I am fine with it."

She didn't know quite what to say to that. However, that was the "bottom line" to it. I just wanted my kids to be happy. And if it makes them happy having both of their parents around, whether they are married or not, then so be it.

I have had some very tumultuous relationships with people in my life. It has been that way with my mom, with both parents relationship-wise. With all of the stepparenting that I have gone through in my life, I just want my kids to feel safe and secure that they don't have to choose one parent over the other. They can love both of us. I have learned a lot from all that I went through.

After dad announced that he was suffering from Alzheimer's disease, TV talk shows started to scramble to have him on their shows as a guest. When dad appeared on *The Tonight Show With Jay Leno*, I couldn't go with him, because the studio audience setup was too small to accommodate a lot of people. Also, Jeremy wanted to go, so Bill got him a ticket, and then Jeremy brought his girlfriend, so that put Bill off. At the same time, Bill had friends coming in from out of town who loved Jay Leno. So, he got tickets for his friends, but he got really pissed off that Jeremy brought a girlfriend. Jeremy is Glen's grandson for crying out loud, but that is just another example of the battles for control that go on in that organization.

I couldn't believe that Bill got really upset just because Jeremy brought his girlfriend with him. But Jeremy has been to plenty of these shows, so he knew that there are always extra seats.

The next TV show that dad was booked on was Jimmy Kimmel's show. Jeremy wanted to go to the taping of *Jimmy Kimmel Live*. So, Cal said to Jeremy, "Well, Bill says he has one ticket and you cannot bring anybody else."

Well, Jeremy has been to *Jimmy Kimmel Live* more than once also, so he knows there's plenty of room there. So Jeremy said to Cal, "Well then fine, I don't need to come. Tell Bill that he can just have my ticket." He wasn't going to play the game.

Bill certainly finds all the tickets he needs to give away to his friends, but he won't let Glen's grandson attend it with a date? That is just another example of the kind of "crap" that started occurring. I think it's just disgusting.

JOURNAL ENTRY / May 2012

I called dad, and had a great conversation with him. We talked about coming to see him in Las Vegas June 1 and 2. I told him that I was bringing his grandkids and his great-grandkids along with my husband and I. He was very excited about that. I told him how I was traveling a lot, and he said, "Yeah, me too. And, I'm sick of it."

I said, "Yeah, but at least you are with family, dad. Now when I am traveling on the road for the airline, I am alone."

He said, "Well, honey, why don't you come back on the road with me?"

I said, "Dad, that is not going to happen, with the-powers-that-be in control of everything. You know that."

He said, "Yeah, with the 'stupid ass' family drama that is going on."

I did however tell him that I was not "fine" with his tour manager, Bill. I had also told him that I had told Bill, "I want to be able to come and see my dad when I want, wherever I want," and that in turn Bill told me that the record company has control over all of the access passes. According to him, they are the ones who decide who gets the "All Access" backstage passes to the shows.

Dad said, "The record company? What a bunch of bullshit! You tell Bill I told him to give you 'All Access' passes for you and my grandkids."

I said, "OK dad."

So the next time I talked to Bill I said, "Dad said he wants us to have 'All Access' passes. And, if you can't say to me that you are going to do it, then let's go up to dad, and discuss it in front of him."

So, Bill told me that he was going to handle it, and of course he never did. He simply put it off. So here I was then in Little Rock, Arkansas, going back to see dad, and I tried to get back and I told the security guard at the backstage entrance, "I'm Glen's daughter, and I need to go back to see my dad."

She said to me, "Well, if you're Glen's daughter, why don't you have a pass?"

It was so embarrassing, I was just fuming inside. I just somehow talked my way through and she let me in. When I arrived backstage I went straight to Bill, and we proceeded to get into a fight about it.

I said, "Bill, I told my dad that you said that I couldn't have an 'All Access' pass because the record company controls all of them."

"I never said that!" he argued very defensively.

"Those were your exact words, Bill," I said. "Would you like to say that in front of my husband, because Tom was standing right there. You said, 'The record company has control over all of the backstage passes,' which I happen to know is a bunch of bullshit."

Since that day, I never got another one. Instead, the next time I was there, I was given a wrist band, like I was just some visitor, or fan, or something.

JOURNAL ENTRY / June 2012

I have become friends with Sarah on Facebook. I am careful of what I say to her, as I know that she talks to Stan. I feel bad for my brother Dillon, as he has always tried to find his way into dad's world too. But little does he know that I always felt like an outsider too. I just hid my feelings a little better.

JOURNAL ENTRY / July 6, 2012

I had a conversation with Kelli on my way to work, that was a great conversation. I can finally talk to her without trying to hide my feelings.

Before now I would keep my thoughts to myself, although I did talk to MaryAnne about all of this. She has been my biggest confidante all of these years.

My husband wants me to talk to a professional, but like I told him and MaryAnne, if I did that they would only hear about my perspective about everything, so how could they give me a valid answer or conclusion. I don't want to come off like a victim or "poor little Debby".

The biggest losses here are mine and dad's. I don't feel a loss about not having Kim in my life anymore. The biggest loss is me and my dad. I have actually grieved for that relationship for a long time. And, I miss Cal. He is a good kid with a big heart, in spite of the "hard ass" persona that he throws out. Shannon and I have never really meshed, nor Ashley and I.

If I have learned anything from all of this, it is that: "Just because you share a parent in common, does not make you a family."

When dad offered me money after the sale of his house in Phoenix, I should have taken that. But I wanted him to set it aside for me, instead of taking it when he offered it. When I lived in Phoenix, I would always fly with dad the day of the show, instead of the day before with the band. I would talk to Kim to make sure that dad had what he needed in his suit-case. I ironed his shirts on the road if they needed it. I told him if it was cold, if it was hot, and what kind of clothes that she needed to pack for him.

When we were at the Andy Williams "Moon River" Theatre, I would sell CDs before and after every show. We would do the first show. After we would come off the stage, then I would go out front and sell CDs. I would come back to the dressing room, and see what he wanted to eat, and then I would go get our food and then I would come back, and we'd eat. I would go back out, I would sell CDs, I would come backstage and change my clothes, and then we would go and do a second show. I would then come back out front and sell CDs after the second show. Dad made a lot of money on all of those CDs that I went out to the lobby and sold.

I have had years of giving and giving without asking for much in return, other than a little respect, and hope that you are loved just because you are loveable. But other people's agendas come into play, and you don't have the power to do anything about it. But I could have said and done some things differently. I could have spoken up around my dad more, and told him more about what I thought about Kim. I just didn't think it was my business. Now when it comes to Kim or dad saying anything about my kids, I had absolutely no problem standing up to either one of them. My kids are now out on their own, making their way in the world and not living off of me or their dad.

I have always supported myself. I still have my airline job, and I have had it all these years. I worked hard and dad was so proud of me. He always told me, "You are the hardest working person I have ever known."

I know my memoir is called *Burning Bridges*, but I don't feel like I am burning bridges. I don't have any more feelings one way or another about some of those folks whom I have spent half of my life with.

In late July of 2012 it was announced that dad was canceling his planned tour dates in Australia and New Zealand, for fear that it might be too much of a strain on him. According to a press release issued to the Australian press, a tour spokesperson was quoted as saying, "Glen is able to comfortably deal with the travel and the shows themselves. However, as August approaches Glen realizes that due to his Alzheimer's condition, he cannot handle the extremely long plane trip from Los Angeles to New Zealand and Australia." When I heard about this, it only made me more concerned about his health.

JOURNAL ENTRY / September 5, 2012

Today we had a gathering of the Clan: the Campbell Clan that is – at my cousin Steve Campbell's home in Arkansas. The event was held so that James Keach and his camera crew could film some things for his upcoming documentary on dad. And of course, dad would be performing at the Robinson Theater in Little Rock tomorrow night.

I wasn't nervous to see everyone, as I have kind of just numbed myself. I toughened up the old hide . . . and heart. I hadn't seen dad since June 2, so I didn't quite know what to expect. It was good. When he saw me, he hugged me and just held me tight.

James Keach asked if he could interview me again and I was very apprehensive about it. I said it probably wouldn't be a very good idea as I still had some unfinished feelings hanging around. He said a little family drama was good. I agreed, and I was very honest with him. He interviewed me again the next day too.

The more I talked the more agitated I became with the whole situation. And it just brought all of those ugly feelings to the surface again. Anyway, we had to cut the interview short today, as they started playing music outside, and it was too loud to do any more interviews. So, we went back outside to visit with relatives.

James wanted dad to visit the cemetery so he could get some shots for the documentary. And of course Kim would go, and Aunt Sandy and Uncle Ed were getting in the truck, and then of course Cal and Ashley. Kelli and I happened to be standing out front, so I said to her, "Hey Sis, let's get in the back of the truck and go watch. So we climbed in the back – with our skirts on no less!

So we arrived there and the crew set up and they started filming some shots. And then dad put his guitar on, and he started playing, and James announced that he wanted dad's family in the shot.

And, that brings me back to the conversation I had with Madi Schneider – God rest her soul – that the only reason I was in dad's life all those years, is that I pushed my way in for our relationship, and my family's. Why is it so very hard to nurture relationships from blended families?

I have some cousins who are gay, and living in Arkansas. They are the sweetest, most loving Christian people I have ever had the pleasure of knowing. They are in church every Sunday, and the whole family is so wonderful, that I wish I lived in Arkansas just to be around such uplifting souls with not a mean bone in their bodies!

I even told James Keach, "If you want to know what it feels like to love and be loved the way Jesus wants for all of us, then these are the people you want to teach you! They are truly amazing and I am so proud they are my family, and anyone who has ever met them will tell you the same."

They have the model *Leave It To Beaver* / Beaver Cleaver life. My aunt and uncle are wonderful people. They love their gay kids and their kids love them. The kids don't want to be around anyone but their mom and dad. It seems like they all spend every waking moment with each other. I truly believe this is the kind of family that every family aspires to be a part of, and to actually know people who live this way is truly inspiring.

When I had this conversation, James Keach said, "Well, I bet they have their moments too."

I said, "Well, I'm here to tell you, they don't. I know that you probably can't believe that they don't, but they *don't*. They are absolutely fabulous."

I was so shocked when dad and Kim were guests on *The Ellen DeGeneres Show* on TV. I have always loved Ellen and watched it every chance I get. Kim would tell me to shut the show off, because her religion doesn't approve of Ellen's openly homosexual lifestyle. So, imagine my surprise when I actually saw her on *The Ellen DeGeneres Show* giving Ellen a big hug.

Unlike Kim's beliefs, if one of my children announced they were gay, I would unconditionally love them. From what Kim has told me, she would not be so open-minded.

I said to my kids, "I hope you forgive me, as your mom, that I didn't short-change you by spending so much of my time trying to have a relationship with my dad. I hope that I did not take away anything from you as a parent, by having an active relationship with my father."

My son Jesse said to me, "Mom, you have shown us what having a family means." And, that made me feel great to hear. Yet, at the same time I know that in a way I did short-change them. I didn't spend every waking moment with them, because I had a job in dad's show, and an airline career at the same time.

I am pretty close to most of my relatives in Arkansas. They are all pretty genuine people; some of the nicest you'll ever meet. Anyone who meets any of them feels truly blessed to be around them all. I know dad loved going home, but I can understand how at times he felt pulled and tugged at as everyone wanted his attention, and it got to be a bit much at times. There was always someone wanting their picture taken with him or having him autograph something. Sometimes we would just have to sneak in so he could just have some "down time" with loved ones. It was just plain hard being him. That's why the moments strolling through the Walmarts or washing clothes while playing cards at the Wash-a-teria Laundromat were such special moments for us both.

When my firing happened, all my uncles and aunts called to tell me how sorry they were, as they knew all these years what I had endured to just be a part of my dad's life.

Let me just say this: my dad is a very simple person with a big heart who loves his family in Arkansas as much as I do. And, I truly believe he wouldn't have made the journey to Arkansas as often as he did if I didn't instigate it so much, since Kim never liked it there, and she wouldn't encourage him to go there. His trips were always my family and his family going together.

JOURNAL ENTRY / September 7, 2012

Here I am on a plane leaving Little Rock; heading home to Phoenix. Last night was very surreal for me. It's been almost a year since the call from Stan telling me that I was fired from the band. "No longer needed" were the words that were used. But that's all "water under the bridge", because it matters not anymore. I did sing onstage with dad last night, and we picked up right where we left off.

It was truly meaningful in my heart, our reunion was fabulous at Steve and LaDonna's home. I hadn't seen dad in three months, and I have a great photo of the show that my cousin snapped when dad saw me. No matter what has transpired, our love for each other will withstand what words cannot express.

But now, as I am writing these words, I actually am finding peace and calm, which I have not felt until this moment. I don't need to be needed anymore in the show. It's OK. I can let go gracefully. I don't have to give James Keach any more stories, because it doesn't matter anymore. And, I know anyone who has been in this family long enough knows the real deal.

I had the great years on the road with dad, just enjoying my life, playing cards, doing crossword puzzles, and playing Wheel of Fortune: simplicity. Just enjoying a wonderful father/daughter relationship: that was my only agenda, and to provide my kids a relationship with their grandparent. So, my sons and daughter also had the best years with dad, and lots of wonderful memories. Everything that we went through to accomplish this only made us stronger and better people – hopefully – for it.

I could have been there, every step of the way, biding my time over-and-over, just to help out with dad. There was plenty of room for all of us, and my brother Dillon – for that matter – is an awesome musician also. And, dad would have loved it as well.

What was going on in dad's life has not gone unnoticed by the news media. Look what's happened to the headlines on the covers of the tabloid newspapers: "Family Rallying Around Glen Campbell Who Has Been Diagnosed with Alzheimer's for a Final Goodbye Tour" said the October

31, 2011 issue of *The National Enquirer*. Inside that issue the publication carried a feature article called "Battle Over Glen Campbell's Fortune" which claimed, "'When Glen's health started failing, Kim saw the opportunity to fire his professional band and his oldest daughter Debby,' divulged a source close to Campbell." Suddenly this whole situation had come under scrutiny of the press.

Relationships are very hard, and family dynamics are even harder. But in mine anyway, I've decided that I can have mutual love and respect for all of the kinfolk, but I don't have to go out of my way to nurture those relationships anymore if it's one-sided. For the 24 years I toured with dad, I had front row seats to see the people who genuinely loved dad. I was his protector, and I can't protect him anymore, it's out of my hands.

Every time I have seen dad, during his 2012 tour, left me an absolute "wreck". My husband can tell you that, and my best friend MaryAnne can tell you that too.

JOURNAL ENTRY / September 21, 2012

Of course I didn't expect to hear from anyone in California for my birthday this year, and I didn't. Dad wouldn't remember, so it wasn't expected. I thought of calling dad on my birthday, but I just never got around to doing it. It just didn't seem that important. I am flying from Philadelphia to Seattle today with about four hours of sleep: tossing and turning, turning and tossing. Life is amazing. One thing that I truly know is that you can't control the outcome. We are all going to die at some time, so the best thing to do is to live each moment surrounded by the people you love more than anything. Then they unconditionally love you back. I have given up on the dream of having a family who loves each other so much that they spend as much time together as they can, and get together as much as they can, where you can actually feel the love every moment you are with them.

Actually, I do have that when I am at home in Phoenix, but not from the people who dad has currently surrounded himself with. Looking back, I have had nearly 24 years of "dad time", during some of dad's best years. We had an incredible relationship, and no one can ever take that from us. So from now on, if I want the perfect world where everyone loves each other so much, and they can't wait to spend time with each other, I will simply have to head down to Arkansas. They truly love each other down there unconditionally. I wanted all of my kids to have that too, and for a time they did. But greed, money and fame destroyed that.

Dad left California years ago, because he wanted a simpler lifestyle. But Kim wanted her kids to be ensconced in the California lifestyle. My sons moved there with them, but my boys wised up and eventually moved away from that environment.

My sister Kelli finally went to visit dad and Kim. I was glad that she is finally spending some time with him. And who knows, maybe she wants to bond with Kim and her siblings.

CHAPTER THIRTEEN

Try A Little Kindness

JOURNAL ENTRY / September 26, 2012

Tears are streaming down my face as I write this, while listening to the song 'Moon River'. I learned today that Andy Williams passed away last night – September 25.

I am recalling all of the wonderful memories at the Andy Williams "Moon River" Theatre in Branson. I know life moves on, but some special memories I just can't seem to let go of, as they were very happy times.

After our shows in the evening, dad and I would usually go to Andy's dressing room and visit with him, and with whomever else was invited. We had so many great times going over to his house, and other times we would go to his brother Don and his wife Jeanne's house, along with Dick and Dee Dee Gass. There are so many great memories of Andy to choose from. Yes I am very sad today. The world has definitely lost a great icon of music, and a nice man. Andy loved my dad for sure. You are missed already Andy! R.I.P.

News travels fast, and when I got wind of the fact that dad was going to play Carnegie Hall on October 13, 2012, I knew that I wanted to be there. It would be the perfect chance to take my daughter Jenny to New York City, since she had never been there. My son Jeremy would simply fly there, and my son Jesse lived there, so we could all be together. We made plans to stay with Jesse, and off we went to New York. I let Stan know that we were coming, and that I was bringing my three kids, and that we were going to come and watch dad at Carnegie Hall, so he arranged to give me tickets.

Since dad has told me he always wants me to sing with him if I can make it to any of the shows, I figured since I was going to New York City with my kids, I would go ahead and sing since it would probably be the last time they got to see me sing with their Grandpa. So I let TJ and Stan know, since I don't care what the rest of them thought about it, as dad always wants to sing his duets, so I didn't need anyone else's permission. Well, of course TJ and Stan mentioned it to Kim and the next thing you know I am getting an e-mail from Stan which read: "I have your tickets for the show and for your family, and you won't be singing with your dad, as this is a big time show and we don't want him distracted, and we don't want anyone backstage before the show so not to confuse him."

Meanwhile, documentary photographer Trevor Albert is back there with his camera filming everything dad does, and more often than not dad was further confused by all of this frenzied film-crew activity around him. This is something I have personally witnessed when I am around him while he is being filmed. They didn't want *me* to be a "distraction?"

Meanwhile I had a guitar that I was carrying along with me. A friend of mine was diagnosed with breast cancer, and Ovation sent me a guitar that I could have signed by dad. It would be raffled off to raise money for my friend and her husband, since they are both flight attendants. He had been by her side in the hospital for the whole ordeal that she was going through. While she was there she almost died, because she caught a virus, and so they were trying to help them live off of the proceeds so that he could remain by her side.

It was such a worthy cause, so I carted this guitar with me from Phoenix all the way to New York City. There was no way that I could watch the show from the audience, especially with the guitar in my lap. My granddaughter Olive was the only person in the family who had a backstage pass. Olive is four years old, so Bill gave her a backstage pass. He had given it to her when dad played New York in 2011. So, Jesse had it, and he made plans to go backstage with Olive.

I said to him, "Well, can you take this guitar backstage?"

And he said, "Mom, why don't you go backstage with Olive, and take the guitar." So, I did.

When I got backstage, the first words out of Stan's mouth were, "What are you doing back here?"

I was more than just a bit irritated by Stan having the nerve to say this to me. I am not a distraction for my father. If anything, I make the mood lighter for him.

I looked at Stan and said, "I am leaving this guitar back here until after the show." Stan was very agitated to see me there. And I was very upset by his behavior too! His own kids would have been upset to hear the way he spoke to me in front of my dad: business manager or not. I belonged since he *was* my dad *first*, before he became superstar "Glen Campbell!" Those are words that should have come from my lips, but of course I kept it in. Well, when my dad saw Olive his face absolutely lit up! He said, "Who is this precious little girl?"

I said, "This is your great granddaughter dad."

He would have rather sat there playing with Olive than to go onstage at Carnegie Hall that night! He loves kids!

I remember one time we were on tour in Canada with a day off so we went to this shopping area to spend the day. Dad wanted some popcorn so we walked over to the movie theater to get some and it was a "Big Kids Day" at the movies.

There were a hundred or so little kids and their parents. Dad went into the crowd and started talking to all the kids in his famous Donald Duck voice. I was so worried some parent would think he was some weirdo talking to their kid. It was quite humorous actually. Dad has no idea how it looks to someone else if they don't happen to know who he is right off the bat.

Anyway, seeing Olive lit him up like a Christmas tree!

I left the guitar backstage and went out and sat down with Olive and next to my sister, Kelli. I sat there watching the show in a trance. I was seeing dad onstage but not hearing anything. I was zoned out: reliving memories in my mind.

I pulled out the note that had been in my tickets, it was a red wrist band printed with the words: "Glen Campbell Goodbye Tour". The note read, "After the show go to side of stage where you will be met by an escort and taken back for a meet and greet with Glen!"

I thought to myself, "Are you f***ing kidding me! So this is what it has come to?"

I knew right then and there this would be the last time I was going to see my dad in concert. I didn't care how many more years they would drag him around, I would not be subjecting myself to that world any longer.

My kids and I went back afterwards with about 40 of his favorite fans, but that is how I have visited my dad since September of 2011. I was either with all of his fans backstage or with 100 or more other Campbells vying for his attention as well.

When I was at Carnegie Hall, I found that I don't even hear the music anymore. I was sitting there thinking, "What the hell just happened to my whole world?"

I am sitting there watching dad perform, and I just blank out, like I am not even sitting there witnessing this. It makes me so sad to see how this has all played out. I kept asking myself, "What is the reason that things have worked out this way? For what?"

I am very disheartened that this is going on. However, I am sure that this goes on in everybody's family. This isn't anything special when you come to think about it. It just happens that dad is a celebrity who is known around the world. However, the dynamics of what is going on just happen to be pretty common from what I have heard. It is very sad.

JOURNAL ENTRY / October 23, 2012 / Part One

I had the most emotionally draining weekend that I possibly have ever had. I flew to Arkansas for the Hot Springs Film Festival, where James Keach and Trevor Albert gave us 34 minutes of unedited clips from dad's documentary on Alzheimer's. I saw the footage of dad and me when I was a young girl, which I had never seen before. So of course that started my tear ducts flowing. And spending time with my loving aunts and uncles and cousins helped. We all got up and sang songs, showing just how talented the rest of the Campbells are too.

Trevor, who is also one of the producers of the documentary, put a microphone in my face and asked me, "So, how do you think that your dad did at Carnegie Hall?"

I said to him, "I don't think that he did very well at all."

Trevor looked shocked, and he said, "Well, that's not how the other people reacted. They only told me about the standing ovation, and the cheering and applauding."

"Well, of course they did," I told him. "He is suffering from Alzheimer's and he is onstage singing. He did a great job for being in the condition he is in. The audience is more than willing to stand up and give him an ovation for the legend that he is, as much as they do for the greatness of his performance."

When we had viewed the documentary that James and Trevor were working on, I have to say that some of it rubbed me the wrong way. On one hand, I have to admit that they tried to get a lot of the significant people in dad's life into it. However, there were a few upsetting surprises in it for me.

When a shot of a lady whom I have never met or seen around the Glen Campbell camp all these years came on the screen, my first reaction was: "Who is this lady?" Then, much to my amazement, she was identified as being: "Glen's publicist". This was even more confusing to me, since I had never laid eyes on her. Sandy Brokaw has been dad's publicist for as long as I can remember, and now here is this lady who I am sure is affiliated with Surfdog, talking about my dad and Alzheimer's disease with tears in her eyes no less!

By no means am I trying to discount how she feels when talking about my dad as there are millions of fans who probably feel the same way she does from growing up with dad's music. However, Sandy Brokaw is dad's publicist and he could truly tell what he feels about all of this because he has been so "up close and personal" to it all throughout the years.

This really upset me. And, that is exactly my point as far as there being absolutely no loyalty in the Glen Campbell Organization whatsoever. And then there was all this footage of them interviewing all these celebrities which – yes – is great as it will help bring more awareness to this horrible disease. But do you see them interviewing Glen's grandkids, who have watched this all take place over the years? No.

I asked James this exact question. In my eyes, if they are just doing this documentary on dad's final "Goodbye Tour", and the struggles of doing the tour while battling this debilitating disease, then why on Earth would you interview Sarah or Tanya as James had hoped to be doing? They have something to do with dad's life, but they have absolutely nothing to do with dad's current struggle.

I totally disagreed with the filmmakers for not having interviewed the people who are actually watching their loved one's mind slip away. In my mind it was nothing short of incredible! Instead, it's all about the wonderful world of making more money and focusing on what really sells!

JOURNAL ENTRY / October 23, 2012 / Part Two

On Sunday morning, following the documentary viewing, my two aunts and two uncles and I headed to Branson for a memorial for Andy Williams. It was held for "invited guests only". I was one of those "invited guests", and I cried practically the whole time. I cried not only for the American icon he was, but also for all of the special memories that dad and I shared there, as well as the rest of the family.

I know you can never go backward in time, but those years I spent in Branson were by far some of the all-time "best years" of my life! And, I can speak for dad also, as I know how he felt there. He loved Branson. The small town atmosphere, and the loving people who lived there at that time, made it very special to us. While I was there I saw so many wonderful friends that we worked with along the way.

Dad didn't go to Andy's memorial service in Branson, because he was on the road somewhere. It sort of amazed me that he would fly back from Ireland to be honored in Nashville on *The Country Music Awards* telecast by Vince Gill, Brad Paisley, and Keith Urban in 2011, but he wouldn't fly into Branson to go to Andy Williams' memorial service.

One of the best friends I made in Branson is Andy Williams' sister-in-law. Don is Andy's brother, and it is Don's wife who I am close to. Don is just a great guy. He is fabulous. Dick and Dee Dee Gass of the Lennon Sisters are also great friends from Branson. I have known them from way back, when the Lennon Sisters would be performing on the same bill as dad, at the Hilton Hotel in Las Vegas. I remember lying out at the pool, and I was babysitting Kelli and Travis and Kane.

Dick and Dee Dee had called me as soon as they heard about my firing in 2011. They said, "Debby, you brought such normalcy to your father." They made me feel real good, and told me that their house is always open to me anytime I want to come to Branson and stay with them. They are just wonderful, wonderful people.

I went to Andy's memorial service with my two aunts. Debbie Williams, Andy's wife, came down the steps to where I was sitting before the memorial got under way, and she came up to me and gave me the biggest hug and said, "I am so sorry to hear about you and your dad. What happened? You were such 'a rock' for him to lean on for all of those years in Branson. And, my friends and I all think it's absolutely disgusting what has happened." Even TJ's mom was blown away to hear how I had been "let go" from the show.

When I got back home to Phoenix, I thought about all of these events: the death and memorial service of Andy Williams, Carnegie Hall, and the film that was being done about dad. It made me wonder how people will think of me when the documentary is finished and screened. I know there are still those people out there who are wondering: "How could Debby have deserted her dad, now that he has Alzheimer's disease, and needs her the most?"

I would have never have deserted my dad. And, now I need to be around him more than ever, because he has Alzheimer's – he is forgetting things. I don't ever want him to forget me, but eventually – if that's the way the disease progresses – then I have no control over anything. I have no control over anything that happens to dad. I hope that I have now set the record straight on that issue. What has happened since September 18, 2011, has all been totally out of my hands.

CHAPTER FOURTEEN

A Better Place

I HAVE so many wonderful memories of my 24 years of being part of dad's show. Although things did turn sour for me, it still cannot color all of the great memories I now have. Along the way I have gotten to meet so many incredible people: some of them famous, and some of them just dear sweet people who have nothing to do with the show–business world at all except for their love of the music.

Through all of my years with dad, I have gotten to know so many of the people who I count as some truly devoted fans who became dear friends. They are fans who I have known for years, and they made the whole experience of singing with dad such a pleasure. Whenever we would go back to one town or another, we would always know that many of these same people would be waiting there to greet us warmly.

I have had a relationship with some of dad's fans that spanned over 40 years. When I was just a teenager and dad performed at the Las Vegas Hilton, I sometimes would wait for the show to be over by spending time in the Teen Club at the Hilton Hotel. One of the mothers who followed dad's show would drop her daughter in the Teen Club also, and I got to know her. So I have basically grown up with the daughter all these years, and she and I have been friends this entire time. It is almost like some of the fans have grown to become part of an "extended family" to me.

I have met their families as well as them meeting mine. It always amazed me how the diehard fans would buy airplane tickets, hotels and car rentals in city after city and spend so much money to follow dad's show all over the world. I was actually floored as I had to basically work two jobs to make ends meet, yet they saved up their hard-earned money just to see dad's shows. I would give some of those fans our complimentary food coupons that dad and I had left over so they could get free meals sometimes. I felt that since they had spent so much money following dad around the country all these years, I should do something nice for them.

Some of the fans would buy me Christmas presents and birthday presents, and they did the same for my kids as well. I would tell them, "Please do not spend money on me." But my words were spoken to no avail.

When they bought dad gifts, if they had purchased the wrong size, or I thought it was maybe something that I knew dad wouldn't use and the money would be wasted, I would always try to get the gifts back to those fans to take them back to the store so it wouldn't be money wasted. Dad has some of the sweetest fans in the world, and they loved my dad with such a loyalty. They had been through all his marriages and the different families too.

I have so many wonderful memories of dad's legion of devoted fans, and through the years they all genuinely meant so much to dad too. He always gave them his time as best he could. He knew what the fans meant for his career. Without them, where would his career be? I have to say that he truly enjoyed spending time with them as well.

One trio of fans we refer to as the Three Amigos – Sandy Gilliard, Lynnie Sadowski and Barb Axworthy – and I have known them for years. I have a really cute a picture of them that dad took, which is in my home office.

Another one of his fans is the wonderful Becky Holman who lives in Missouri. She is the most awesome cake maker on the planet! OMG! I would have her make all the birthday cakes that we had at the theater in Branson.

Then there is my special friend Will, who lives in Scotland. He actually had a picture of dad tattooed on one of his arms, and dad's autograph tattooed on his other arm. Will is such a wonderful, down-to-earth man whose wife, Liz, actually knitted beautiful sweaters for my granddaughter Olive when she was born.

Then there is Seth Golding and his wonderful family from Ohio; Hyde Kirby and his wife Ilene from Philly; and Michelle Rich who actually lives in Phoenix. She and Hyde are still to this day moderators for an internet site that is known as the Forum. It is a site where Glen Campbell fans can go and discuss everything about dad and anything connected to dad, including us kids. There are some quite magnificent things you can find on this site.

The list of fans who became friends of mine goes on and on: Vicky and Bud Johnson; Kevin Lemons; Arlene (AR) Wunsch, who is always letting me know about some great Glen Campbell collectible items! They are mostly in her house – ha ha! Then there is Barb Keifer, and Dolores, Kathy Schick and Ged Fitzgerald!

Truly all of the fans that were there for dad all these wonderful years and for me as well, I just thank them all from the bottom of my heart. I know that there are countless names that have slipped my memory, and if I were to write them all down, that would be a book in itself.

JOURNAL ENTRY / January 15, 2013

My relationship to my sister Kelli has always been up and down, but the book that I am writing is not about this. Even though I was singing with dad, I tried to include her in everything that was going on, and I think our relationship really changed after her mom, Billie, died. Although I remained in their lives – in some capacity – it was never quite the same once Billie was gone. They were as screwed up as I was about trying to figure out where they fit into dad's life. But their mom's death afforded them their way out of the chaos.

I remember sitting on Billie's deathbed, pouring my heart out to her, and Kim calling me and telling me I had no reason to be there in California. But, yes, I needed to be there for Billie, and for Kelli, Travis and Kane. I went with them to Carlsbad to bury their mom. I was even included in the obituary, by Lilly, Billie's mom. I have loved all of my half brothers and sisters, but sometimes I think to myself: "You just can't pick your family."

Dad has never gone out of his way to be part of any of our lives. We have always had to be the ones reaching out to him. And I reached out for 24 years. I don't know what went on with Travis and Kim, for Travis to have stayed away all of this time. I have seen things that he has written, so I have an idea. After I got fired from the Glen Campbell Organization, Travis did reach out to me, picking my brain a lot, about certain things pertaining to business – like dad's royalties and such. But I have no clue about any of this.

I don't have any clue what Kelli, Travis and Kane have gotten from their mom's will or trust. Travis was thinking I had been a part of Billie's will. I have no clue how it turned out, as it is none of my business.

JOURNAL ENTRY / February 20, 2013

I am very sad for the loss of my friendship with Bill and also Stan. Bill has been like a brother to me and we shared some great memories over the years. I always tried to help in any way I could to make things easier for him while we were out on the road. Sure, we had disagreements, but I used to have the utmost respect and love for him. I watched this transformation of a wonderful caring man to someone who became cold and calculating, a shell of the businessman I once knew. This was especially true with Julian Raymond in the picture, and then later with Surfdog Records. He wasn't in control of the Glen Campbell Tour anymore and he was not too happy for that. I remember when I showed up in London in October of 2011, he said he was going through the same crap, with the young band members showing up late to the bus all the time. According to him, they had no respect for the tour rules, and there was too much partying all the time now, and beer was flowing quite generously on the bus. And mind you they are *all* on one bus, with dad, drinking and carrying on.

And, the way Bill treated me after that just got worse. He even cut me off of the website where I could go to find where they were on the road and which hotel, so I could call and talk to my dad when I wanted. These days dad no longer has a cell phone of his own, so I was at the mercy of Kim's phone if I needed to talk to him, and I will never dial her number again!

The lost relationship with Stan hurts the most, since he was my biggest confidante. All the things confided in him I should have been saying to my dad all these years. He would have been so angry. In addition, all the things Stan confided in me could have had a big impact too.

Stan has been around for a long time. He had been in the picture for over 40 years I believe, so he was like an uncle to me. I know the whole Schneider family. Stan and I have gone through years and years of great memories together.

I had an overnight airline flight in Orange County one year, and Stan picked me up and took me to an Angels baseball game. We sat and watched it together in country legend Gene Autry's suite at the stadium. Stan was close friends with Gene and his wife, Jackie, and he handled all their affairs for many years as well. Dad was good friends with them too. I had the pleasure of meeting Gene several times.

This photo was taken when we were on the bill with two popular country singers, Trace Adkins and Neal McCoy. Of all the performers I have gotten to know, Neal is one of the best. He is such a wonderful person and a great entertainer.

My sons Jesse (left) and Jeremy (right) with dad and me. When this photo was taken we were all on our way to The Country Music Association's induction of dad into its Hall of Fame.

When dad and I were on tour in Australia, we had a night off and we went to see Trisha Yearwood doing a special promotional show there at the time. This was years before she married Garth Brooks, and before she became a TV cooking star.

This was the last picture of me and my dad, my kids, and grandkids all together in April of 2011, at his house in Malibu. We were gathered there for his 75th birthday. Not pictured is my husband Tom and grandson Micah, as they were running around the house somewhere.

This photo was taken on my first tour to the Gold Coast in Australia. Here are dad, myself and his long-time manager Stan Schneider.

When dad headlined The Troubadour in West Hollywood, Tanya Tucker came by and asked us to get her into the show to see dad's "Meet Glen Campbell" show. Here she is clowning around with my son Jesse while I look on from the right. She has been an important part of dad's life, and she really is a very nice person.

Initially, Kim didn't tour with dad often, but the frequency did increase as time went on and particularly after her three kids joined in dad's act. Here I am with dad and Kim, waiting for the train to Newcastle during a tour of the British Isles.

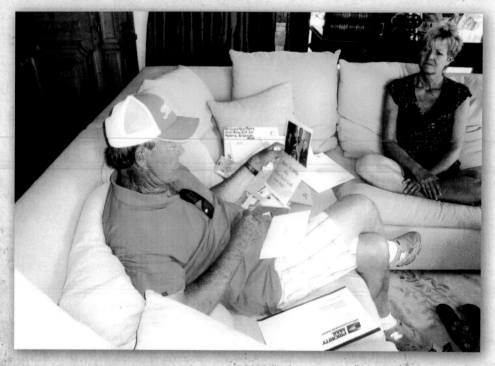

Here I am with dad on his 75th birthday in 2011. Instead of fans sending dad e-mails, I asked them to send him actual birthday cards that he could open on this milestone day.

Of all of dad's eight children, I am the one who had the chance to tour with him for 24 consecutive years. I was with him for some of his greatest career triumphs, and I now have a lifetime of incredible memories to look back upon.

This was taken at a special fundraiser show, held in Branson when George Bush Sr. was campaigning to be President of the United States. Left to right: one of the Baldknobblers, dad, Jim Stafford, George Bush Sr., Box Car Willie, Barbara Bush, Loretta Lynn and myself.

Dad was often booked to do private parties and corporate events. This picture was taken at someone's ranch outside of Sacramento, California.

When I would go and visit dad in Malibu, he would always want me to go golfing with him and his buddies. That is his friend Dante Rossi in the yellow shirt between us.

Dad and I with two of our best friends, Martha and John Hanna. This photo was taken in Branson. The four of us spent a lot of time golfing together.

Dad's longtime band and staff: Bill Maclay (tour manager), TJ Kuesnster (musical director), dad, Brad Conyers (stage sound), me, Kenny Skaggs (guitar, vocals), Russ Skaggs (bass), Richard Landers (house sound), Gary Bruzzesse (drums, vocals), and my son Jeremy who sometimes came to hang out with us.

I never had any personal ambitions in the music industry. The only reason I went out on the road to sing with dad for 24 years was the fact that I wanted to have a genuine father-daughter relationship with him. Moments like this are now among my favorite memories.

Well, those are all times that are long gone. It is all very sad. They reached out to me when I first was let go from the G.C. Organization, and now I hear nothing from them. I am OK with it though.

I also recently heard from Dillon. He wanted my side of the story, and not some trumped-up version from someone on the other side of the family in California. After I told him what went down, he voiced his opinion on all of it. I haven't heard from him since.

I know that Travis doesn't gel with Kim, from his dealings with her in the past. Kelli hasn't come around all these years. Kane has been away all these years, in and out of prison. He is a good kid with a big heart. I wish I could help him more.

Dad has definitely been an "absentee father" to all of them, except to Cal, Shannon and Ashley, and of course he is married to their mom.

And, me: I pushed my relationship with dad. I freely admit it. How sad is that, to have to push and insist that I have a relationship with a parent? It is just supposed to happen naturally – I thought.

Dad has lived around so much chaos and construction for the last 25 years. Every house that dad and Kim have lived in has been torn apart. They have built two recording studios, and torn apart three houses.

I have been privy to at least three conversations with dad and Stan, where Stan told him point-blank that he should curtail spending on the houses, or he isn't going to have any money left.

Dad's comment was, "Well, when it's gone, it's gone."

Of course, Stan would jokingly say, "When you suddenly can't buy the next, best, world's greatest golf club, then what?"

Then I heard dad agree, and say, "Then I had better tell Kim to curtail her spending immediately."

After I was so unceremoniously fired from dad's show, I cut off all communication with Kim, Ashley, Cal, and Shannon, as well as Stan and Bill, and anyone who is still part of the inner circle. I wasn't talking to anyone.

Since all of this happened, Kim and dad sold the Malibu, California, house, and they have since moved to somewhere else in Malibu. *The Los Angeles Times* reported that it sold for $4.45 million.

I have no idea where the house is located, as I have never been there. Thankfully they kept the same house phone number so I could call, and sometimes dad would answer, but other times Kim would, and I would simply ask to speak with dad. Or I would have my husband call Kim's cell phone and get dad on the phone for me.

My brother Cal did text me in 2013, after New Year's, to say, "I love you big sis, I hope you know that. And I love your boys, and please give my love to Tom, Jenny, and Morgan."

I also spoke to dad in January 2013. I happened to be in Honolulu, and Steve Ozark was there. He knew dad back in the days that Billie was around. He phoned dad at his house, because he was going to visit dad and stay at the house with him. So, we called dad from his phone when I was with Steve.

As of January 2013, dad is fine, but he is not doing well. This is just what I surmise from talking to him on the phone. I certainly haven't spent any quality time with him since I left the show in 2011. Aside from meeting him backstage after shows, and getting a hug here and there, I really haven't been with him in person.

There was a little family reunion before one of the Arkansas shows, and I got to spend a little time with him. But the camera crews were busy filming him, so there was very little interaction between just he and I.

On August 13, 2013 a new album of music by dad was released, entitled *See You There*. It was assembled from "outtakes" from the *Ghost On The Canvas* album. It was again done with Julian Raymond's involvement. It was assembled from "stripped down" tracks of dad singing many of his greatest hits, and three songs credited as being co-written by dad and Julian Raymond. This time around, it was Kim who was listed as the Executive Producer of the album, and she wrote the liner notes.

I think that by getting this all out on paper, whether it is in a book for anybody to read, or if it is just for myself, I found that I just had to get it all out in black and white, and get it out of my head. I am organizing this book as much to just see all of the facts in front of me, as much as I am letting the public in on this.

I could go to a therapist and pay out countless hundreds of dollars to get this out of my system, or I could write this book. This way I am able to get all of these thoughts out of my system once and for all, and be done with it.

I have my friends, like my best friend MaryAnne, and my own family to serve as a sounding board for this. These are people who I trust to give me the bottom-line truth about the mixed emotions that I am going through.

If the stories that I have told on these pages are merely figments of my imagination, MaryAnne and my husband, Tom, would have told me. Instead they are 100% supportive that I am doing the right thing by drawing the conclusion that I have reached as to what is going on. If I had done anything to deserve what has happened to me, and the way that I was fired from my father's show, MaryAnne and Tom would have told me.

If there is someone out there who is reading this book, and has a parent who is suffering from Alzheimer's disease, I have something to say to them specifically: "If you ever have anything in your heart that you have held inside, for fear that you would make waves, get it out. Everybody is "worth it" in this life. Everybody has feelings that they harbor. Everybody should be validated. If there is something that you have to say to your Alzheimer-suffering parent, please tell them. Clear the air while they can still grasp what it is that you are saying, and what it is that you are feeling.

I never wanted to be a person who has felt that they have taken advantage of any situation. Whenever dad would offer me money, I would always say, "No, dad. I am OK, I am working. I have health insurance. Just put that money for me and my kids for later. I don't need it now."

When my dad offered me his personal jewelry, and much of it was very valuable, I didn't want to take it. I told him, "No dad, you are still living, and you have seven other kids too. Maybe we will all pick out our favorite piece of jewelry at some point."

There were two rings that dad had made years ago. One of them had his name spelled out in diamonds, which he gave to me, and the other one was a banjo-shaped ring encrusted with diamonds, which Cal has.

I said to Cal one night, while we were out on the road, while Ashley was sitting there, "You should give the banjo ring to Ash since she plays the banjo and it will mean more to her."

Ashley replied, "I just like diamonds."

My jaw just dropped open. Ashley just didn't seem to get it at all. Really? "I just love diamonds?" I had to just let that comment go as well. What is done is just done.

My relationship with my mom is fine right now. It is not strained or anything. I think that we have an OK relationship. I try to call her whenever I can. She and Jack live right here in Phoenix, but I don't see her a lot. I always see her on holidays and on special occasions. I try to talk to her at least once a week, and I make every effort to do that. My relationships with my mother and my father are very different.

While I have gotten the short end of the stick – so to speak – by being fired from dad's show, I am also appreciative for what I have had. None of my other siblings have had quite the same relationship with dad that I have had.

No matter what occurs from this point forward, they can never turn back the hands of time, and have the kind of fun and the kind of quality time that I have spent with dad. None of them will have that unique kind of relationship with him that I have enjoyed. I have so many wonderful memories of the traveling that we did around the world, and the adventures we have had.

When it comes down to the question of where do I go from here, I can first of all say that I am facing a future of being fine with the way things are. I am perfectly OK with what my dad and I were about for 24 years. I know how he felt about me. The June before I got fired I had a message on my phone: "Hi, this is Glen Campbell, your daddy, and I'm just calling to tell you I love you." My dad made it a point to call me and tell me how much I meant to him when he had all of his faculties about him. He was the kind of dad who would just call to say: "Hi honey. I just called to see what you are doing. How are you doing?" to me.

By saying that, I am not in any way gloating. I would hope that any of my seven siblings would have the same relationship with him, and to feel that kind of love from dad. My sister Kelli holds it against me that I was able to sit with her mom, and tell her mom – Billie – how I felt when she was on her deathbed.

I told Billie how I was told what I could and could not do as far as she was concerned. I told her all about the ultimatum that dad had laid on me about never talking to Billie again. I was so glad that I made my peace with Billie at the end. Kelli was never able to make peace with her mom, so maybe she has held that against me all of these years. Who knows what she is thinking. I can't be worried about what everyone else in the family is thinking. You can't do that in life at all.

All I can control is me, and what I have done with my life, and all of the crap that I have done with my life. All I know is that I gave my all to my dad for all those years. I will always love him, just because he is my dad. I

148

never cared whether or not he was "Glen Campbell" the singing star. That has nothing to do with anything. I didn't care what he did for a living, I just loved him for being my dad.

I feel good about my life, and the decisions that I have made. And I also feel good about having put all of my thoughts together in this book. I don't care what anybody else thinks in that world. I had a great relationship with my dad that no one else had, with no ulterior motive.

Ever since dad's public disclosure of having Alzheimer's disease, I have heard from an amazing number of supportive people. One of these has been Tanya Tucker. I have to admit that I never really knew Tanya very well at all. It's really funny: I would never set myself above anybody, so therefore anybody who reached out to me, I allowed it. I was pleasantly surprised that Tanya really reached out to me after I met her. I ran into her a couple of times, and she has always been very warm and friendly towards me. And – of course – she had always been in love with my dad.

I know that some people might think, "Now why would I suddenly be friendly with my dad's ex-girlfriend?" I look at Tanya as a caring friend, and I was happy when she got in touch.

Tanya reached out to me right after she heard that dad had Alzheimer's disease. She was very sweet and concerned. Tanya said to me, "I've written your dad a letter, and I would like to get it to him."

I told her, "I will try to get it to him for you."

She wanted to make amends for everything that they had been through together. So I let her in, and somehow things got all convoluted. Whatever dialogue that went on after that was out of my hands. As far as I could see it, an old friend wanted to reach out to dad, and I assisted in getting her in touch with him. End of story.

I wasn't really actively in dad's life while his affair with Tanya was going on. Since I was in Italy at the time of their very public relationship, I have very little knowledge as to what all was going on between the two of them. So when Tanya contacted me, I could only get so far in the middle of helping to patch up whatever it is that they went through together.

I have been a pretty screwed-up person because of all that has transpired. I have made a vow to myself not to be screwed up anymore.

I have a life and an identity apart from my dad's life, and I know who I am. Because I am suddenly not in the "show business" realm, I am not lost at all. Performing with dad was just fun for me, because it became a bond for the two of us. Singing is something that I have always loved to do. I miss doing that to a degree, but what I miss the most is dad.

I was not defined by being "Glen Campbell's daughter". I am defined by being both of my parents' daughter, regardless of what profession they had.

It has not been an easy road to travel the past couple of years. I go to work every single day, and not a day goes by without someone saying to me, "How is your dad doing?" And, I can't really give them an accurate answer, but I do. I say, "He's doing OK" or I say, "Well, it's a little rough, but thanks for asking." I find that I just have to make polite innuendos about it, because I really don't know how dad is anymore.

And, as much as I try to get it out of my head every single day, dad is not far from my thoughts. When people ask me if I am singing anymore, I just tell them, "No, I am retired."

I am asked about my life in the show-business world, every single day. There is no getting around it, and it is fine. But at the same time it is sad to me. I just have to find my happy medium mental space in the middle of it all. I can't let it upset me.

I am so happy to be writing this book, maybe I can just get on with my life, and not let thoughts of worrying about what my dad is going through dominate my life.

Do I want to sit there in a room with dad, and have him go, "Who are you?" No, not really. That would be like a knife going in me to have that happen. If things didn't work out the way they did, I would be facing that. I would have gone through that, but now that I am out of dad's circle, I am spared that.

However, if dad suddenly called me and said, "Come here, I really need you," I would be there. And if dad suddenly decided he wanted to be here in Phoenix, I would say to him, "Dad, come live with me." My husband and I would absolutely take care of him.

Since they sold the Malibu house in early 2013, I don't even have an address for dad. Kim claims that she has been downsizing, to make it easy for Glen. At least that's what I have heard in all of the interviews.

There has been such an outpouring of love for him, from people around the world, and it is great for me to know how much dad and his music have touched so many. Looking back at his music catalogue, if I had to choose my favorite of all of his songs, it would be 'I Will Never Pass This

Way Again', from the 1972 album, *Glen Travis Campbell*. It was a song about living life to the fullest. Dad was such a great story teller, and such a great ballad singer. He really put his all into that song.

He might have done the *Meet Glen Campbell* and *Ghost On The Canvas* albums recently, but I never really gelled with those albums. Those weren't the kind of albums that really represent his music to me. He got talked into those albums more than anything. He would have been better off doing an all-Jimmy Webb album instead of *Ghost On The Canvas*.

He would probably have loved to reunite with Jimmy Webb for one last album. I think that would have been better for him commercially, and artistically.

Jimmy is also one of his friends who first began to notice the signs of dad's Alzheimer's disease. He ran into my dad at the Ryman Auditorium in Nashville a couple of years before the diagnosis, and dad walked up to him and said, "Did you write 'Wichita Lineman?'" Jimmy was at first deeply hurt that my dad could forget something like that. Webb had written three of the biggest songs in dad's career – "By The Time I Get To Phoenix', 'Wichita Lineman' and 'Galveston' – and they recorded a whole studio album together in the seventies. However, after that incident he realized dad had a serious problem going on.

In 2012 Jimmy Webb played at a charity gig in Malibu at the home of actress Jane Seymour, and he commented about dad, "He played a couple of guitar solos at Jane Seymour's that had my mouth hanging open. The kind of jazz improvisational style – the guitar picker – is pretty much unimpeded in him. It would be silly to say he plays the right licks. He plays inspired licks."

According to Jimmy, "Glen is never more active than when he's got his guitar in his hands. He knows what he's doing. The fingers remember."

If I had anything to say about it, I would put dad and Jimmy Webb in the recording studio for one more album together. I think it would do dad a world of good. Unfortunately, I don't have anything to say about this.

With all that has been going on in my life, I have come to rely on my closest friends more and more. In March of 2013 my dear friend MaryAnne Beaman wrote me a sweet and supportive letter to give me encouragement about what was going on in my life. In this letter she wrote: "As time went on and you traveled more and more with your dad and became a permanent part of your dad's show, I saw you take on many roles, a singer, a mom with an unbelievable schedule, a best friend and caretaker (in the best sense of the word) to your dad, an event organizer to the crew, and a genuine friend to all including fans, employees and venue staff. Not everyone was accepting of this, especially in the later years when the dynamics of the Glen Campbell Organization had changed. I saw you and your feelings become a bit callused. That saddened me greatly because that is not the core being of who you are. This is where I saw you struggle the most: Do you just 'go with the flow', or be your caring self, that somehow left you in a position of great hurt and angst?

"We've had many conversations about your mom and your dad and how you have had to find a way into both of their lives and make it as important to them as it is to you. That is just you. I know you have struggled with siblings, band members, G. C. employees, stepmothers, family and family friends to find your place within each of the situations. Some of these times have been good, and some have been hurtful. Despite the difficult feelings presented to you by all in your life, you have been able to find a place where you belong in your dad's heart. I must say you have also reached and touched the hearts of many fans that have loved you and your dad for many years. They call you 'friend' and vice versa. You have been able to nurture and combine Glen Campbell, the international famed superstar, and the very normal dad role for you and your dad, and in return you have enjoyed a person that loves you – both as his eldest daughter and best friend. Glen certainly relied on you for many things and one of those is being a best friend. How nice is that?! Many could only wish for that in a lifetime."

Another dear friend and airline co-worker, June Sovay, recently wrote a piece about me that I found especially encouraging. In part it read: "Debby Campbell loves with her heart and soul. Don't ask her to love you if you don't want to be loved completely and forever . . . I spent more time in those years watching this woman wrestle with her own marriage, her children, her work and her life than I spent watching over her finances. From the moment she spilled her soul to me I knew front and center that she loved her dad . . . She devoted time to reflecting on past family relationships and her role and responsibility, hoping to provide something more for her own small family unit, and hoping as well to provide some sort of family cohesiveness born out of the dysfunction of the past. She was on an overnight in one of our California cities where her dad was performing, and that was the night she stepped onto the stage and in front of the audience professed her love for her dad, sang with her dad, became a public figure with her dad; and, it was there that the healing of some of the familial wounds began. It was a pivotal moment for both of them . . . It was pivotal because Glen Campbell became the father Debby Campbell had always wanted. She spent the last 25 years doing what she thought was important, not what her friends told her was important. And, as a result she was able to give herself to her dad as a daughter, she was rewarded with a real father, she accumulated for her children a family, tradition, and memories that will last a lifetime."

I feel so encouraged to know that none of the upset that I have felt in the last few years is at all unjustified or self-imposed. I makes me happy to know that at the end of the day, I have done all I could for my dad all these years.

I struggle every day about calling Kim but – ultimately – I don't do it. I don't want to be drawn into that world again. Although now that dad isn't on the road anymore we will have to come to some sort of an agreement, so that I can visit my dad and he can spend some time with his grandkids and great-grandkids also.

That is just one of many things that have happened lately. And, dad has no idea. He doesn't know anything about what is truly going on behind the scenes. Trust me when I say, if he did suddenly recognize what was actually happening, all *hell* would break loose.

And, if he knew how I cry night after night about what has transpired since 2011, he would be heartbroken.

I can truly say: I never had an agenda with dad. I really never had any aspirations of trying a singing career. It was my friend MaryAnne and Holly (Bill Maclay's wife), who actually came to me and said that they would like to manage me. They thought I had a shot at a career in singing. I never really had much confidence in myself but if they thought I did, then I was willing to try. They would book me here and there, and we even did a showcase at Douglas Corner in Nashville. I was so very nervous and dad of course came to support me.

We eventually went to Branson and started a live morning show, which was staged at what was then called the Roy Clark Theater. It was a struggle to build a fan base with the ever-changing audiences, but we kept on trucking onward. For a while we were one of the only morning shows in Branson, and certainly there were enough tourists in town to support it every day. The other one was hosted by Bob Nicols. Since that time many more have started up in Branson.

With everything that is going on at the moment, I tried to have a relationship with all of the kids – my siblings – as best I could. But everybody's trying to find their own way into their own relationship with dad.

My brother Kane is now out of prison, and has been doing really good, and is reaching out to me. He needs to see dad, as he hasn't seen him in a long time. We have been talking about how we can make that happen.

Hell, here I am trying to find a way that I can see my own father, and Kane is calling me and wanting me to be the one to help him do the same thing. Kane had a lot of problems when dad and Billie divorced, and he got involved in drugs and stealing, and forging checks out of his mom's account. I don't know the exact extent of what he did do, nor did I know the reason why he stayed there for years, but he had a lot of stuff going on in his life that he couldn't handle.

I wasn't privy to everything that went on in Kane's life at the time. When dad wrote his own book in 1994 he revealed, "As [Billie] lay dying . . . one of my children, Kane, stole things from her house and sold them to buy drugs. He, at the same time, wrote checks on her account and forged her name. The infractions were the latest in a long series in Kane's life. He was arrested at the funeral. I have spent money into seven figures on Kane's counseling. I don't know how much responsibility to feel for his situation. I know I was an absentee father."

I felt so bad for Kane, but he stayed in prison for several years.

When Billie's kids started questioning me about all of this stuff going on in the office of the G.C. Organization, after I was no longer a part of it, I told them, "I don't know anything."

After Billie's death, I was "nothing" in Kelli's eyes. That was pretty much the demise of the closeness – or lack of it – that existed with those three siblings. Even though I went with them and helped them bury their mom in New Mexico, I haven't felt a real closeness since then. However, I am happy to know that Billie's mom loved me, and she included me in the obituary that appeared in the local paper; listing me as one of Billie's daughters.

I don't talk to Stan anymore. That is sad, but that is fine I guess. Bill

Maclay – dad's tour manager – I couldn't give two cents about knowing what is going on in his life. When I was with the organization, Bill was like my brother, and I loved him. It's just sad to see it all play out the way that it is unfolding.

What is going on at the moment, is that everyone is jockeying for position. It is pretty sad to watch all of this happen.

Now that I no longer have the outlet of singing with dad, lately, I have been thinking about getting back in singing. I've been talking to my manager/business partner/best friend, MaryAnne. She and another friend have talked me into dabbling in singing solo, possibly on some cruise ships, or other gigs like that. We shall see. I don't know what will transpire, but you never know, it might be a lot of fun.

My singing professionally was mainly an avenue as to a way to get to know and spend time with dad. I was so disheartened when I was let go by dad's organization, I was content to just drop it all. Now maybe it is time to revive my singing career. I am definitely contemplating it.

I wouldn't be going out with the intent of having a huge career, I would like to just go out and have some fun with it. I have always loved to sing, and maybe that is going to be my way of feeling like this is all a new beginning.

I have a job still, with the airlines, so maybe this will be my hobby. I am always singing at work, and my co-workers will say, "So, why don't you go out and sing still?" I have to admit that I love music, and I miss singing, because it's a big part of my life.

It is also part of my kids' lives too. My granddaughter Morgan, who is 17, has a beautiful voice, but I think it is doubtful she will want to go into singing. Her brother, Micah, however, is always moving to the beat. He absolutely loves music. I bought him a drum set and when he is maybe a year or two older, I will get him lessons. When we are in the car he will be singing along with Jason Aldean, or whoever is on the radio at the time. He will say, "Nana, turn it up!"

I remember one day around Christmas season, he and I were wearing Santa hats and singing carols as we shopped, he all of a sudden just blurted out in song: "Just like a rhinestone cowboy." I just cracked up when he did that! My granddaughter, Olive, is five and she is such a beauty. I am so very blessed with my kids and grandkids. So very thankful!

Dad just loves kids. I have a great picture of him and his three great-grandkids. He loves them all. It is sad that they don't get to see him as much as they did before all of this happened.

My relationships to date with all of my siblings continue to be as different and varied as we all are. I don't see myself reaching out to Kelli anymore, as I have done in the past, as it has always been me doing all the work. One thing I will say however, is we always seem to pick up right where we left off.

I used to think her and I would be OK, but it seemed the closer dad and I got, she would pull away. I even took Kelli to Cabo San Lucas, Mexico, one year with my other sister Denise, best friend MaryAnne and our four boys. We had so much fun! I have a lot of love for Kelli in my heart, but I can't continue to give my all anymore. It zaps me. I just want her to be happy.

Travis and I did not speak much over the years I sang with dad. He did come to Branson for dad's 60th birthday party that I had arranged. And after his divorce from Andrea he came to a show once with his new wife Trudy. Travis did contact me after the "firing" as did a lot of people. But I definitely know Travis' pain as he is a child of divorce also, and not being around dad much and his mom gone, well one could only imagine. So I can definitely relate. And I love him and his wife Trudy is very nice.

Kane is out of prison, doing very well "staying clean". I talk to him weekly and really need to make a point of seeing him. He has a good support system I hear, so I am glad. He has only seen dad once, however.

I try to talk to Dillon often, and I did have dinner with him and Sarah recently. I had "an overnight" in Los Angeles and they came and had dinner with me. He is busy writing music and recording and working on projects with his mom. He has definitely been left out the most. But, if he ever needed me, I would be there and I hope he knows that.

I wish I could have helped him with dad more, but I was so busy trying to find my way, and my kids' way, it never occurred to me.

As far as Cal, Shannon and Ashley go, they were more like my kids than my brothers and sister. Cal at least has reached out to me, so I know he has a heart and feelings. I wish all of them success with their careers.

I will say I am the only one of dad's kids who has consistently worked all these years. I wish all of them the best life they can possibly have!

I try and go see dad when I can, and call him when I can, and that is the extent of our relationship now. It is like it came around full circle.

By putting all of my thoughts and feelings on these pages, it has been somewhat a catharsis for me. This is the first time my kids will read what my journey has been like and hopefully they will have a better understanding of my thoughts and feelings. But most of all, I want them to know how very proud I am of all three of their lives through all of this too!

My daughter Jenny is in the dental field and has owned her own home since she was 21. She has beautiful children: Morgan and Micah. My son Jesse graduated from Scottsdale Culinary Institute with honors, and is a "wonderful" chef at a top restaurant in the West Village of New York City. He has beautiful Olive as a daughter, and is a wonderful dad! My son Jeremy is a model/actor living in Los Angeles. As I stated at the beginning of this book: You are all my heart! I am so very proud of all of you!

I have since talked to Stan. I actually called him a couple of weeks ago. I told him he disappointed me the most of all. He was very apologetic and admitted to me that he was wrong. He told me that I belonged anywhere my dad was and that my kids do too. And anytime I am in California to please call and come see him. So I guess I am at peace with our relationship although I somehow know it will never be the same.

As for Kim, she has once again put their house that she bought about nine months ago up for sale, and if it goes through her and dad will move to Nashville where her kids and Shannon and Ashley are.

The only comfort I get in that potential move is that he will be closer to Arkansas and his brothers and sisters will be within driving distance to see him. He is slowly slipping away from all of us. I had lunch with him a couple of weeks ago. It was arranged for me to meet him for lunch at Malibu Country Club after his golf game. I took my granddaughter Morgan with me, and we rented a car once landing in Los Angeles. We drove up to Malibu, where my son Jeremy and his girlfriend met me.

When we got there Dad looked at me with those sparkling blue eyes and gave me the biggest, tightest hug. I said, "Do you know who I am?"

"Of course you're my baby girl," he said. But he did not know who his great granddaughter was, but he knew he loved her. His memory was slipping as far as knowing his grandson too. Jeremy does go to their house on occasion, but dad is slipping away memory-wise day by day. It was a good lunch with much of the conversation in "repeat mode".

For instance, he said to Morgan, "Who do you belong to?"

And he said to me, "Now where do you live these days?"

However, just being there with him for that short hour was wonderful. I don't know when I'll see him again especially if they move to Nashville. But I know I will somehow, someway. I am sad. So sad, my heart breaks.

Maybe it is time to no longer take care of everyone else, and finally take care of Debby for a change. Now I don't have to worry about everyone else in the family.

Sometimes it hurts, but now it is time for me to heal. I don't want to be that person anymore who thrived on being needed. I need somebody to need and want me in a way that unfolds and evolves naturally. I was always the one who wanted to be the fixer, but this family nonsense is something that I cannot fix. I found all of this so frustrating, and I am finished with the constant frustration.

All of the animosity that I have felt has started to dissipate. I just have to release it and let go of it all.

So, if anyone wonders why I wrote this book: It's an incredible story of how I stayed in my dad's life against all odds, and loved him no matter what the cost. And, no one can ever take my truly wonderful memories away.

I have been a constant in dad's life one way or another through all the wives, the divorces and the sibling rivalries. When I think of how I was pushed aside it really is astounding to me. How very sad that it happened the way it did!

My life has been a daughter's journey to find her way into her father's life through many trials and tribulations. 'Burning Bridges' was the very first song I sang onstage with my dad at the Arizona State Fair in 1987. It is also the last two words I heard from Stan when I was let go from dad's Goodbye Tour. His words still distinctly ring in my ears: "Debby, don't burn bridges."

Well, if this book burns some bridges – so be it. The whole purpose of writing it was to chronicle how a child from divorce can find her way back into the life of her beloved but estranged father. For 24 years I succeeded in an amazing way. I will continue to see dad whenever I can. My love for him will never diminish.

Debby Campbell's Family Tree

HER FATHER'S MARRIAGES AND CHILDREN:

Glen Campbell [Father] (Born: 1936)   Diane Kirk [Mother] (Born: 1940)
Marriage: 1954 to 1959
Children: Glen Travis Campbell Jr. [Brother / Deceased]
(1955–1955)
Debby Campbell [Self] (Born: 1956)

Glen Campbell   Billie Jean Nunley [Stepmother #1]
Marriage: 1959 to 1976
Children: Kelli Campbell [Half-Sister]
Travis Campbell [Half-Brother]
Kane Campbell [Half-Brother]

Glen Campbell   Sarah Barg Davis [Stepmother #2]
Marriage: 1976–1980
Children: Dillon Campbell [Half-Brother]

Glen Campbell   Kim Wollen [Stepmother #3]
Marriage: 1982–present
Children: Cal Campbell [Half-Brother]
Shannon Campbell [Half-Brother]
Ashley Campbell [Half-Sister]

Glen Campbell Discography

ALBUMS

GLEN CAMPBELL / STUDIO ALBUMS:

Big Bluegrass Special (with Green River Boys)
1962, Capitol

Too Late To Worry, Too Blue To Cry
1963, Capitol

The Astounding 12-String Guitar Of Glen Campbell
1964, Capitol

The Big Bad Rock Guitar Of Glen Campbell
1965, Capitol

Burning Bridges
1967, Capitol

Gentle On My Mind
1967, Capitol
(Number 1 US Country / Number 5 US / Number 3 Canada)
US: Platinum

By The Time I Get To Phoenix
1967, Capitol
(Number 1 US Country / Number 15 US / Number 24 Canada)
US: Platinum

Hey, Little One
1968, Capitol
(Number 1 US Country / Number 26 US / Number 24 Canada)
US: Gold

A New Place In The Sun
1968, Capitol
(Number 1 US Country / Number 24 US)

Bobbie Gentry & Glen Campbell (with Bobbie Gentry)
1968, Capitol
(Number 1 US Country / Number 11 US / Number 8 Canada)
US: Gold

That Christmas Feeling
1968, Capitol
US: Gold

Wichita Lineman
1968, Capitol
(Number 1 US Country / Number 1 US / Number 1 Canada)
US: 2× Platinum

Galveston
1969, Capitol
(Number 1 US Country / Number 2 US / Number 4 Canada)
US: Platinum

True Grit (Film Soundtrack Album)
1969, Capitol
(Number 77 US)

Try A Little Kindness
1970, Capitol
(Number 4 US Country / Number 12 US / Number 12 Canada)
US: Gold

Oh Happy Day
1970, Capitol
(Number 16 US Country / Number 38 US / Number 38 Canada)

Norwood (Film Soundtrack Album)
1970, Capitol
(Number 36 US Country / Number 90 US)

The Glen Campbell Goodtime Album
1970, Capitol
(Number 2 US Country / Number 27 US / Number 23 Canada)

The Last Time I Saw Her
1971, Capitol
(Number 6 US Country / Number 87 US / Number 84 Canada)

Anne Murray / Glen Campbell (with Anne Murray)
1971, Capitol
(Number 4 US Country / Number 128 US / Number 12 Canada)

The Artistry Of Glen Campbell
1972, Capitol

Glen Travis Campbell
1972, Capitol
(Number 5 US Country / Number 148 US)

I Knew Jesus (Before He Was A Star)
1973, Capitol
(Number 13 US Country / Number 154 US)

I Remember Hank Williams
1973, Capitol
(Number 10 US Country / Number 205 US)

Houston (I'm Comin' To See You)
1974, Capitol
(Number 12 US Country)

Reunion: The Songs Of Jimmy Webb
1974, Capitol
(Number 18 US Country / Number 166 US)

Ernie Sings & Glen Picks (with Tennessee Ernie Ford)
1975, Capitol

Rhinestone Cowboy
1975, Capitol
(Number 1 US Country / Number 17 US / Number 7 Canada)
US: Gold

Bloodline
1976, Capitol
(Number 2 US Country / Number 63 US / Number 58 Canada)

Southern Nights
1977, Capitol
(Number 1 US Country / Number 22 US / Number 4 Canada)
US: Gold

Basic
1978, Capitol
(Number 17 US Country / Number 164 US)

Highwayman
1979, Capitol
(Number 19 Canada – RPM Country Albums Chart)

Somethin' 'Bout You Baby I Like
1980, Capitol

It's The World Gone Crazy
1981, Capitol
(Number 49 US Country / Number 178 US)

Old Home Town
1982, Atlantic
(Number 33 US Country)

Letter To Home
1984, Atlantic
(Number 30 US Country)

No More Night
1985, Word

It's Just A Matter Of Time
1985, Atlantic
(Number 32 US Country)

Still Within The Sound Of My Voice
1987, MCA
(Number 32 US Country)

Light Years
1988, MCA
(Number 58 US Country)

Favorite Hymns
1989, Word

Walkin' In The Sun
1990, Liberty

Unconditional Love
1991, Liberty

Show Me Your Way
1991, New Haven
(Number 19 US Christian)

Rock-A-Doodle (Animated Film Soundtrack Album)
1992, Liberty

Wings Of Victory
1992, New Haven
(Number 22 / US Christian)

Somebody Like That
1993, Liberty

Home For The Holidays
1993, New Haven

The Boy In Me
1994. New Haven

Christmas With Glen Campbell
1995, Laserlight

A Glen Campbell Christmas
1998, TNN Classic Sessions

My Hits And Love Songs
1999, EMI

Love Is The Answer: 24 Songs Of Faith, Hope And Love
2004, Universal South

Meet Glen Campbell
2008, Capitol
(Number 27 US Country / Number 155 US)
[Debby Campbell appears on this album]

Ghost On The Canvas
2011, Surfdog
(Number 6 US Country / Number 24 US)

Glen Campbell And Jimmy Webb In Session (with Jimmy Webb)
2012, Fantasy

See You There
2013, Surfdog
(Number 22 US Country / Number 89 US)

GLEN CAMPBELL / LIVE ALBUMS

Glen Campbell Live
1969, Capitol
(Number 2 US Country / Number 13 US / Number 6 Canada)
US: Gold

Live In Japan
1975, Capitol

Live At The Royal Festival Hall
1977, Capitol
(US Country 23 / Number 171 US)

Glen Campbell Live
1981, RCA/Energy

Glen Campbell Live! His Greatest Hits
1994, Laserlight
[Debby Campbell appears on this album]

Glen Campbell In Concert (with the South Dakota Symphony)
2001, Columbia River

GLEN CAMPBELL / GREATEST HITS AND COMPLIATION ALBUMS:

[Only the major compilation albums are listed, as dozens of compilation albums have been reissued during Glen's career]

Glen Campbell's Greatest Hits
1971, Capitol
(Number 3 US Country / Number 39 US)
US: Platinum

Christmas With Glen Campbell
1971, Capitol

Arkansas
1975, Capitol

The Best Of Glen Campbell
1976, Capitol
(Number 11 US Country)

Glen Campbell's Twenty Golden Greats
1976, EMI

Glen Campbell: 20 Golden Hits
1978, EMI

The Great Hits of Glen Campbell
1978, Capitol

The Glen Campbell Collection
1978, Capitol/TVLP

Country Boy
1983, Capitol

Glen Campbell: All Time Favorite Hits
1984, Capitol Special Markets

The Night Before Christmas
1984, Capitol

Favorite Songs Of Inspiration
1985, Capitol

Country Favorites By Glen Campbell
1985, Capitol

The Very Best Of Glen Campbell
1987, Capitol

Phoenix and Other Favorites
1990. Capitol

Love Songs
1990, EMI Gold

Country Gold
1991, Capitol

My Best to You
1991, Capitol

The Essential Glen Campbell Volume One
1995, Capitol

The Essential Glen Campbell Volume Two
1995, Capitol

The Essential Glen Campbell Volume Three
1995, Capitol

Glen Campbell: Super Hits
2000, Atlantic

20 Greatest Hits
2000, Capitol
(Number 71 US Country)

Glen Campbell: All The Best
2003, Capitol
(Number 12 US Country / Number 89 US)

Rhinestone Cowboy: The Best Of Glen Campbell
2003, EMI

The Essential Glen Campbell
2003, EMI

Glen Campbell: The Legacy (1961–2002) [4-CD Boxed Set]
2003, Capitol
[Debby Campbell appears on this album]

Glen Campbell Sings The Best of Jimmy Webb 1967–1992
2006, Raven

Glen Campbell: The Platinum Collection
2006, Rhino

Classic Campbell
2006, EMI

Glen Campbell: Platinum
2008, Capitol

Glen Campbell: Live in Concert
2008, Acrobat

Glen Campbell: Greatest Hits
2009, Capitol
(Number 63 US Country)

Glen Campbell: Duets
(with Bobbie Gentry, Anne Murray, Rita Coolidge, Tennessee Ernie Ford, Tanya Tucker)
2009, Micro Werks

Glen Campbell: Limited Edition: 2 CD Set
2011, Curb
(Number 69 US Country)

Glen Campbell: Icon
2013, Capitol
(Number 61 US Country)

SINGLES

1958
Dreams For Sale (With The Glen-Aires)
I Wonder (With The Glen-Aires)

1961
Winkie Doll (As Billy Dolton)
Valley Of Death
Turn Around, Look At Me
Buzz Saw (As The Cee Gees)

1962
The Miracle Of Love
Too Late To Worry, Too Blue To Cry
Long Black Limousine
Kentucky Means Paradise (With The Green River Boys)

1963
Prima Donna
Dark As A Dungeon (With The Green River Boys)
Same Old Places

1964
Through The Eyes Of A Child
Summer, Winter, Spring And Fall

1965
Tomorrow Never Comes
Guess I'm Dumb
Universal Soldier
Private John Q

1966
Can't You See I'm Trying
Burning Bridges

1967
I Gotta Have My Baby Back
Gentle On My Mind
By The Time I Get To Phoenix

1968
Hey Little One
I Wanna Live
Dreams Of The Everyday Housewife
Gentle On My Mind (Re-Release)

Wichita Lineman
Mornin' Glory (With Bobbie Gentry)

1969
Let It Be Me (With Bobbie Gentry)
Galveston
Where's The Playground Susie
True Grit
Try A Little Kindness
Honey Come Back
All I Have To Do Is Dream (With Bobbie Gentry)
Oh Happy Day
Everything A Man Could Ever Need
It's Only Make Believe

1971
Dream Baby (How Long Must I Dream)
The Last Time I Saw Her
I Say A Little Prayer / By The Time I Get To Phoenix (With Anne Murray)
Oklahoma Sunday Morning

1972
Manhattan, Kansas
I Will Never Pass This Way Again
One Last Time

1973
I Knew Jesus (Before He Was A Star)
Bring Back My Yesterday
Wherefore And Why

1974
Houston (I'm Comin' To See You)
Bonaparte's Retreat
It's A Sin When You Love Somebody

1975
Rhinestone Cowboy
Country Boy (You Got Your Feet In LA)

1976
Don't Pull Your Love / Then You Can Tell Me Goodbye
See You On Sunday

1977
Southern Nights
Sunflower
God Must Have Blessed America

1978
Another Fine Mess
Can You Fool

1979
I'm Gonna Love You
California
Hound Dog Man
My Prayer

1980
Somethin' 'Bout You Baby I Like (With Rita Coolidge)

Hollywood Smiles
Any Which Way You Can

1981
I Don't Want To Know Your Name
Why Don't We Just Sleep On It Tonight (With Tanya Tucker)
I Love My Truck

1982
Old Home Town
I Love How You Love Me

1983
On The Wings Of My Victory
Letting Go

1984
Faithless Love
A Lady Like You

1985
(Love Always) Letter To Home
No More Night
It's Just A Matter Of Time

1986
Cowpoke
Call Home
Another Day In America

1987
The Hand That Rocks The Cradle (With Steve Wariner)
Still Within The Sound Of My Voice

1988
I Remember You
I Have You
Light Years

1989
More Than Enough
She's Gone, Gone, Gone

1990
Walkin' In The Sun
On A Good Night

Somebody's Leaving
Unconditional Love

1991
Living In A House Full Of Love
The Greatest Gift Of All (With Russ Taff)
Right Down To The Memories

1992
Jesus And Me
Where I Am Going
The Eyes Of Innocence
Somebody Like That

1993
Searching Love
I Will Arise

1994
The Best Is Yet To Come
The Boy In Me
Mansion In Branson

1995
Come Harvest Time
Living The Legacy
No More Night

1997
Call It Even

GLEN CAMPBELL / GRAMMY AWARDS

2012
Lifetime Achievement Award
Glen Campbell

1968
Album Of The Year
By The Time I Get To Phoenix
Glen Campbell, Artist. Al De Lory, Producer.

1967
Best Vocal Performance, Male
By The Time I Get To Phoenix
Glen Campbell, Artist.

1967
Best Contemporary Male Solo Vocal Performance
By The Time I Get To Phoenix
Glen Campbell, Artist.

1967
Best Country & Western Recording
Gentle On My Mind
Glen Campbell, Artist. Al De Lory, Producer.

1967
Best Country & Western Solo Vocal Performance, Male
Gentle On My Mind
Glen Campbell, Artist.

GLEN CAMPBELL / FILMOGRAPHY
FILMS:

True Grit (1969)
Starring: John Wayne, Glen Campbell, Kim Darby, Robert Duvall, Dennis Hopper
Glen Campbell role: LaBoeuf

Norwood (1970)
Starring: Glen Campbell, Kim Darby, Joe Namath, Carole Linley, Pat Hingle, Dom DeLuise, Meredith MacRae
Glen Campbell role: Norwood Pratt

Rock-A-Doodle (1991)
Animated film featuring the voices of: Phil Harris, Glen Campbell, Christopher Plummer, Sandy Duncan, Ellen Greene, Dee Wallace
Glen Campbell role: Chanticleer

GLEN CAMPBELL / TV SHOWS:

The Glen Campbell Goodtime Hour (1969–1972)
Weekly Variety Series starring Glen Campbell (1969–1972), John Hartford (1969–1972), Anne Murray (1970–1972)
Guest Stars included Bobbie Gentry, Linda Ronstadt, John Wayne, Dionne Warwick, Lily Tomlin, Jerry Reed, the Osmond Brothers, Paul Lynde, Dom DeLuise
Head Writer: Steve Martin

The Authors

DEBBY CAMPBELL is a singer and performer, who sang professionally for 24 years with her celebrated father, country singer Glen Campbell. She sang and performed for many years with Glen in Branson, Missouri, at several theaters during the nineties, including a run of several years at the Glen Campbell Goodtime Theater. She appeared as Glen's opening act for countless concerts, and was known for singing both solos and duets in her father's show. She was also his opening act for several years. Debby can be heard on the Glen Campbell albums *Glen Campbell Live! His Greatest Hits* (1994), *Glen Campbell: In Concert* (2001), *Glen Campbell: The Legacy [1961–2002]*, and *Meet Glen Campbell* (2008). She is married to Tom Cloyd, and they live in Phoenix, Arizona. This is her first book.

MARK BEGO is the author of 61 published books on rock'n'roll, country music, and show business. He is a professional writer who is called "The Number One Best-Selling Pop Biographer" in *Publisher's Weekly*, and has been referred to in the press as "The Prince of Pop Music Bios". With over 10 million copies of his books in print, Bego has written two *New York Times* best-selling books (*Michael!* [Jackson] and *Leonardo DiCaprio: Romantic Hero*), and a *Chicago Tribune* best-seller (*Dancing in the Street: Confessions Of A Motown Diva* with Martha Reeves of Martha & The Vandellas).

Mark recently returned to magazine writing for Event Bookazines. He and Mary Wilson together authored the publication *50th Anniversary Celebration: My Supremes / Mary Wilson* (2012) and in 2013 he wrote *Leonardo DiCaprio: Movie Idol*.

He has also written books with several rock stars, including Micky Dolenz of the Monkees (*I'm A Believer*), Jimmy Greenspoon of Three Dog Night (*One Is The Loneliest Number*), Debbie Gibson (*Between The Lines*), Freddy Cannon (*Where The Action Is!*), and Randy Jones of the Village People (*Macho Man*). His most highly acclaimed books include

Aretha Franklin: Queen Of Soul, Linda Ronstadt: It's So Easy, Billy Joel: The Biography, Cher: If You Believe, Elton John: The Bitch Is Back, and *Madonna: Blonde Ambition.*

In 2010 Bego published his rock'n'roll memoir, *Paperback Writer,* which includes his adventures and encounters with Mary Wilson, the Village People, Michael Jackson, and Madonna. It won awards at the Paris Book Festival and the Hollywood Book Festival in 2013. His 2012 international book, *Whitney Houston: The Spectacular Rise And Tragic Fall Of The Woman Who Inspired A Generation,* was the first book to chronicle the pop diva's shocking death. As his 60th book Mark published his first novel in 2012: *Murder At Motor City Records,* which critics have claimed is: "a wonderful read . . . it's like 'Agatha Christie Goes to Motown!'" and "What if *Dreamgirls* was a murder mystery, and all of the singing stars on the label are the murder suspects?" It won an award at the Paris Book Festival in 2013.

Mark's books on the stars of country music have included *Patsy Cline: I Fall To Pieces, Country Hunks* (Garth Brooks, Brooks & Dunn, etc.), *Country Gals* (Reba McEntire, Dolly Parton, etc.), *George Strait, Alan Jackson,* and *Vince Gill.*